W9-AHS-100

GREAT MILITARY LEADERS
of the 20TH Century

DOUGLAS MACARTHUR
MAO ZEDONG
GEORGE S. PATTON
JOHN J. PERSHING
ERWIN J.E. ROMMEL
H. NORMAN SCHWARZKOPF

GREAT MILITARY LEADERS
of the 20TH Century

ERWIN J.E. ROMMEL

EARLE RICE JR.

INTRODUCTION BY
CASPAR W. WEINBERGER

SERIES CONSULTING EDITOR
EARLE RICE JR.

CHELSEA HOUSE
PUBLISHERS
A Haights Cross Communications Company
Philadelphia

FRONTIS: Rommel with Kesselring

CHELSEA HOUSE PUBLISHERS

VP, NEW PRODUCT DEVELOPMENT Sally Cheney
DIRECTOR OF PRODUCTION Kim Shinners
CREATIVE MANAGER Takeshi Takahashi
MANUFACTURING MANAGER Diann Grasse

STAFF FOR ERWIN J.E. ROMMEL

EXECUTIVE EDITOR Lee Marcott
PRODUCTION ASSISTANT Megan Emery
PICTURE RESEARCHER Sarah Bloom
SERIES & COVER DESIGNER Keith Trego
LAYOUT 21st Century Publishing and Communications, Inc.

A Haights Cross Communications ✦ Company

http://www.chelseahouse.com

First Printing

1 3 5 7 9 8 6 4 2

Library of Congress Cataloging-in-Publication Data

Rice, Earle.
  Erwin J.E. Rommel / by Earle Rice, Jr.
    p. cm. -- (Great military leaders of the 20th century) Includes index.
Summary: Describes the life and career of Erwin Rommel, field marshal under Hitler during World War II, who is particularly remembered for his role in the campaign in northern Africa.
  ISBN 0-7910-7405-6 (hardcover)
  1. Rommel, Erwin, 1891-1944--Juvenile literature. 2. Marshals--Germany--Biography--Juvenile literature. 3. World War, 1939-1945--Campaigns--Africa, North--Juvenile literature. [1. Rommel, Erwin, 1891-1944. 2. Generals. 3. World War, 1939-1945--Germany. 4. Germany--History--1933-1945.] I. Title. II. Series.
D766.82R43 2003
940.54'23'092--dc21

2003007320

TABLE OF CONTENTS

INTRODUCTION

by Caspar W. Weinberger

At a time when it is ever more apparent that the world will need skilled and bold military leaders, it is both appropriate and necessary that school history courses include studies of great military leaders.

Democracies, for the most part, are basically not greatly interested in military leadership or military matters in general. Fortunately, in the United States we have sufficient interest and volunteers for military service so that we can maintain and staff a very strong military with volunteers—people who want to serve.

That is very fortunate indeed for us. Volunteers and those who decide of their own free will that they want to be in the military are, generally speaking, easier to train, and to retain in the services, and their morale is markedly higher than that of conscripts. Furthermore, the total effect of a draft, based on our Vietnam experience, can be very bad—indeed it can polarize the country as a whole.

One of the best ways of ensuring that we will continue to have enough volunteers in the future is to study the great accomplishments of our past military leaders—the small group of leaders and others who contributed so much to our past greatness and our present strength.

Not all of these leaders have been Americans, but the

example that all of them set are well worth studying in our schools. Of the six military leaders chosen by Chelsea House's "Great Military Leaders of the 20th Century," I had the privilege of serving under and with two.

In World War II, after two years of volunteer service in the infantry at home and in the Pacific, I was transferred from the 41st Infantry Division then in New Guinea, to General Douglas MacArthur's intelligence staff in Manila, in the Philippines. One of my assignments was to prepare drafts of the general's daily communiqué to other theatre commanders around the world. This required seeing all of the major military cable and intelligence information, and digesting the most important items for his daily report to the other war theatres of the world. It also required a familiarity with our plans to carry the war to the enemy as soon as sufficient strength had been transferred to our theatre from Europe.

The invasion of Japan toward which all the planning was aiming would have been a very difficult and costly operation. Most of the tentative plans called for landing our force on one of the southern Japanese islands, and another force on Honshu, north of Tokyo.

We know that Japan's troops would have fought fiercely and very skillfully once their homeland was invaded. In fact, all of our plans forecast that we would lose virtually all of the first two U.S. divisions that landed. That was one of the main reasons that President Harry Truman concluded we had to use the atomic bomb. That ended the war, and all landings taken in Japan were peaceful and unopposed.

Many years later, when I was secretary of defense under President Ronald Reagan, a part of my duties was to recommend generals and admirals for various U.S. and NATO regional commands. Fulfilling this duty led me to interview several possible candidates for the post of commander in chief of our Central Command, which had jurisdiction over our many military activities in the Middle East.

My strong recommendation, accepted by the president, was that he name General H. Norman Schwarzkopf to lead the Central Command. A short time later, General Schwarzkopf led our forces in that region to the great military victory of the Gulf War.

General MacArthur and General Schwarzkopf shared many of the same qualities. Both were very experienced army officers tested by many widely different conditions all over the world. Both were calm, resolute, and inspirational leaders. Both were superb military planners and developers of complex and very large-scale military operations. Both achieved great military successes; both had the best interest of all our troops at heart; and both were leaders in the best sense of the word. They both had the ability and skills necessary to work with military and civilian leaders of our allies and friends in all parts of the globe.

It is vitally important for our future as a democracy, a superpower and a country whose strengths have helped save freedom and peace, that our children and our schools know far more about these leaders and countless others like them who serve the cause of peace with freedom so well and so faithfully. Their lives and the lives of others like them will be a great inspiration for us and for later generations who need to know what America at its best can accomplish.

The other military leaders whose lives are presented in this series include a German, General Erwin Rommel, and the former Communist China leader, Mao Zedong.

General Rommel won many preliminary battles in the desert war of World War II before losing the decisive battle of El Alamein. He had to develop and execute his tactics for desert fighting under conditions not previously experienced by him or his troops. He also became one of the masters of the art of tank warfare.

Mao Zedong had to train, develop, arm, and deploy huge numbers of Chinese soldiers to defeat the organized and experienced forces of Chiang Kai-shek's Nationalist government. He accomplished this and, in comparatively short time, won the military victories that transformed his country.

Both of these generals had to learn, very quickly, the new tactics needed to cope with rapidly changing conditions. In short, they had to be flexible, inventive, and willing and able to fight against larger opposing forces and in unfamiliar environments.

This whole series demonstrates that great military success requires many of the qualities and skills required for success in other fields of endeavor. Military history is indeed a vital part of the whole story of mankind, and one of the best ways of studying that history is to study the lives of those who succeeded by their leadership in this vital field.

CASPAR W. WEINBERGER
CHAIRMAN, *FORBES* INC
MARCH 2003

CASPAR W. WEINBERGER was the fifteenth U.S. secretary of defense, serving under President Ronald Reagan from 1981 to 1987, longer than any previous defense secretary except Robert McNamara (served 1961–1968). Weinberger is also an author who has written books about his experiences in the Reagan administration and about U.S. military capabilities.

1

"The Officer's Way"

*A*t age 52, the field marshal was recovering nicely at home in Herrlingen. The wounds that he had received almost two months earlier would have killed most men, yet he had survived. His iron constitution and fierce will to live had carried him through the dark, pain-filled hours when death had lingered close to his bedside, beckoning. He had fought hard for life and he had won. More recently, perhaps invigorated by the crisp autumn air, he had even allowed himself to look forward to a full recovery. But that was before the Führer's (leader's) agents arrived at his home at midday on October 14, 1944.

■   ■   ■

Nicknamed "The Desert Fox," Field Marshal Erwin Rommel earned a reputation as a fierce soldier and expert military strategist – serving as commander of German forces in North Africa during World War II.

The field marshal's son Manfred arrived in Herrlingen at 7:00 A.M. on October 14, 1944. Now 15 years old and an antiaircraft-gun crew member in the Luftwaffe (German Air Force), he had been given a day's leave to visit his father. He joined his father for breakfast. Afterward, they strolled together in the family garden. The boy's father spoke first. "At twelve o'clock to-day two Generals are coming to see me to discuss my future employment," he said. "So to-day will decide what is planned for me; whether a People's Court or a new command in the East."[1]

"Would you accept such a command?"[2] the boy asked.

His father explained that Germany's enemy in the East was "so terrible that every other consideration must give way before it."[3] He went on to say that should the Soviets overrun Europe, even for a short time, everything that makes life worth living would end. In answer to his son's question, he replied, "Of course I would go."[4]

Just before noon, the field marshal went to his room on the first floor and changed from a brown civilian jacket that he usually wore over riding breeches to a tunic that he had worn in the *Afrika Korps* (Africa Corps). He favored the tunic over some of his other uniform coats because of its open collar. Then he slipped his *Pour le Mérite*—now chipped and dented from the accident— over his head and positioned it at his throat. The medal was his nation's highest award for valor. He now felt ready to meet his visitors.

The two generals arrived promptly at noon in a dark-green Opel sedan bearing a Berlin license plate. Their driver parked the Opel in front of the garden gate. Besides father and son, the only other men in the house were Captain Hermann Aldinger, a reserve officer who had served on the marshal's staff in North Africa, and Rudolf Loistl, a badly wounded war veteran who was then serving as the marshal's soldier-servant.

A bell jangled at the front door. Rudolf answered it and ushered in the two generals—the first large and red-faced, the second a bit shorter with a long, pointed nose and foxlike ears. A third officer, a major, followed them into the foyer. Lucie, the field marshal's wife, invited them to stay for lunch. The first general politely declined. "This is official business,"[5] he explained, requesting permission to talk privately with the field marshal.

The marshal, appearing to the generals to be momentarily relieved, escorted his visitors into his first-floor study. The major stepped out into the garden to wait. Turning to his aide, the marshal said, "Have the Normandy dossier ready, Aldinger!"[6] Meanwhile, Manfred went upstairs to find a book to read while waiting for the visitors to leave.

Captain Aldinger left to fetch the dossier, then joined the major in the garden. The two officers chatted for a while, reminiscing about the Dresden Infantry School, where the major had once studied under the field marshal. While they talked, Rudolf walked down to the Opel to invite the driver to pull it through the gate. The driver shook his head no. "That doesn't make sense,"[7] Rudolf said.

The driver retorted, "*Kamerad* [Comrade], you do what you're told and I do what I'm told."[8] His icy demeanor surprised Rudolf. Before returning to the house, he glanced down the street and saw another, larger car that appeared to be waiting.

After almost an hour, the long-nosed general came out of the study and joined the major in the garden. Shortly thereafter, the field marshal and the red-faced general emerged. The marshal went upstairs to Lucie's bedroom, while his visitor stepped out into the garden with the others.

Upstairs, the marshal conferred briefly with his wife. Manfred could hear sounds of their muffled conversation. Moments later, the marshal exited Lucie's room and called for Rudolf to summon Manfred. After another moment or two, he sent his son after Aldinger. The aide bounded up the stairs carrying the Normandy dossier.

In 1944, Rommel was implicated in a plot against Hitler and was made a grim offer by his Führer: face trial for treason or choose "the officer's way."

Waving the dossier aside, the marshal said, "I won't be needing it—they came about something quite different."[9] Downstairs, the generals waited.

The field marshal descended the stairs. Rudolf helped him on with his topcoat and handed him his cap and field service baton. The marshal shook hands with his staff, turned, and strode out the door with the two generals into the bright October day. Captain Aldinger and Manfred hurried down the path with the marshal.

When the group reached the Opel, the marshal spoke briefly to Captain Aldinger and Manfred, then handed his house keys and wallet to his son to look after. Manfred would later recall marveling at his father's composure. When the marshal turned to enter the Opel, the red-faced general stiffened and saluted him in the obligatory Nazi fashion. *"Heil Hitler!"*[10] he said. The marshal climbed into the rear of the car, followed by the two generals. The sedan then ascended the small hill beside the house and disappeared around a bend in the road.

Manfred watched the Opel until it rounded the bend. His father did not look back. Field Marshal Erwin J.E. Rommel had been offered a choice by his Führer—and he had chosen "the officer's way."[11] Manfred returned to the house to find his mother.

2

"A Useful Soldier"

After the establishment of the German Empire in 1871, a career as an army officer started to become fashionable in Germany, even among middle-class southern Germans without a military tradition in the family. One of that era's more noteworthy middle-class aspirants to a career in the military was Erwin Johannes Eugen Rommel.

Born on November 15, 1891, in Heidenheim an der Brentz, Württemberg, to a schoolteacher father and a mother who was the daughter of a senior official, Erwin Rommel was one of five children. Although frail and small of stature, he showed an early determination to succeed at whatever he set out to achieve. Later, his father, in recommending his 18-year-old son

Rommel's early military training began in 1910 at the War Academy in Danzig (now Gdansk, Poland). It was while seeking a commission in Danzig that Rommel met Lucie Maria Mollin, the woman who would become his wife and lifelong partner.

for military service, described Erwin as "thrifty, reliable, and a good gymnast." [12]

On July 19, 1910, Erwin joined the Imperial German Army's 124th Württemberg Infantry Regiment as an officer cadet. After passing prerequisite courses for the enlisted ranks of corporal and sergeant and completing the course at *Kriegschule* (War Academy) in Danzig (now Gdansk, Poland), Cadet Rommel received his commission as a *Leutnant* (second lieutenant) in January 1912.

In evaluating Rommel, the academy's commandant noted, in part, that he was "of medium height, thin, and physically rather awkward and delicate," but mentally "well endowed" with "a strict sense of duty."[13] In ending his singularly unspectacular appraisal, the commandant concluded that Cadet Rommel would make "a useful soldier."[14]

While seeking a commission in Danzig, Rommel also found his life's partner and only woman in his life— Lucie Maria Mollin. Of Polish-Italian descent, she was the dark and alluring daughter of a Prussian landowning family. She was studying languages in Danzig when Rommel met her. The two would eventually marry, but Rommel would first need to establish himself in his chosen profession. He returned to his infantry regiment in Weingarten, near Stuttgart, to begin practicing the techniques of command.

The 124th Infantry (also known as the Sixth Württemberg) was quartered in an ancient monastery, and it was with a monk-like devotion that Rommel applied himself to his new duties. For the next two years, he drilled recruits while war clouds gathered over Europe. After a brief posting to a field artillery regiment in Ulm, near his hometown, he returned to the 124th on July 31, 1914, to find the monastery bustling with activity.

Three days earlier, Austria-Hungary had declared war on Serbia, ostensibly in retaliation for the assassination of Archduke Franz Ferdinand and his spouse by a Serbian national in Sarajevo, the capital of Bosnia, on June 28, 1914. The assassination of the heir to the Austro-Hungarian throne did not, by itself, cause the outbreak of hostilities, but it set in motion a complex chain of actions, reactions, and military mobilizations that soon raged out of control. Simply put, Europe split along lines of long-standing alliances: the Central Powers, chiefly Germany and Austria-Hungary; and the Allied Powers, or Allies, mainly France, Great Britain, and Russia (and later, the United States). And the opposing factions entered into the so-called Great War (World War I).

On August 1, Rommel's regiment was outfitted with field equipment. That night, the regiment assembled for inspection in field-gray uniforms. After a stirring speech, the regimental commander announced the mobilization. "A jubilant shout of German warrior youth echoes through the ancient gray walls of the monastery,"[15] Rommel wrote later in *Infanterie Greift An* (*Infantry Attacks*), his book on tactics. Desmond Young, one of Rommel's biographers, points out that "such comments sound less like Rommel than a gloss by a Nazi propagandist, preparing a 1937 edition for popular consumption."[16] (Nazi was short for *Nationalsozialist*, or National Socialist German Workers' Party, the political party of German dictator Adolf Hitler.) In any case, the 124th Infantry Regiment went off to war the next day, jubilant perhaps, but innocent and untested.

Rommel's blooding—that is, his first exposure to enemy fire in combat—came on August 22, 1914, during the German advance on the Marne River. While leading an early morning reconnaissance patrol near Longwy, France, his platoon drew enemy fire. Rommel halted his platoon and entered the farming village of Bleid with an advance party of three men. Rounding a bend in the road leading to a farm, the four men ran into a group of twenty French soldiers. Faced with his first command decision, Rommel reacted as he would on many future occasions. Counting on surprise, he attacked!

Firing on the run, Rommel and his three men routed the Frenchmen before they could collect their wits. Rommel then called up the rest of his platoon and proceeded to clear and raze the village. Bleid, in Rommel's words, soon became a blazing inferno of "thick, suffocating smoke, glowing beams and collapsing houses."[17] He accomplished this while suffering from a severe case of food poisoning. It was a minor affair of little importance,

Rommel's first combat experience came during a German advance on France's Marne River in August 1914. When his advance party of four encountered a group of twenty French soldiers, Rommel chose to attack, surprising and defeating his enemies. Here, French forces cross the bridge at Marne.

except that it demonstrated Rommel's characteristic independence and boldness.

On September 24, while engaging in sporadic fire-fights in a wooded area near Varennes, Rommel came face to face with five Frenchmen. Shooting two and missing a third, he found his magazine empty. Without hesitation, he fixed his bayonet and charged the remaining enemy. Suddenly, a French bullet struck him in the left thigh, carving a hole the size of a balled fist. It was his first battle wound. Rommel survived the incident and received the Iron Cross, Second Class, at the base hospital in Stenay a few days later.

Rommel returned to action in the Argonne forest in January 1915 to find that the war of movement had settled into a war of static entrenchments. It was still war, however, and Rommel was becoming quite good at war.

On September 29, he led his platoon through barbed wire into a French fortification and captured four enemy blockhouses. He later repulsed a French battalion-size counterattack, then withdrew with the loss of fewer than a dozen men. Rommel's reputation for leading from the front was growing throughout his regiment. "Where Rommel is," his troops said, "there is the front."[18] This episode earned him an Iron Cross, First Class.

In late June 1915, Rommel's battalion revisited the same locale where he had fought on January 29. He engaged in a further action in which he sustained a second leg wound, this time from shrapnel in the shin. After a short spell in the trenches, Rommel was promoted to *Oberleutnant* (first lieutenant) in September and posted to the newly forming *Württembergische Gebirgsbataillon* (Württemberg Mountain Battalion). This unit, larger than a regular battalion, comprised six rifle companies and six mountain machine-gun platoons. When deployed, it usually separated into two or more elements called *Abteilungen* (battle groups) as dictated by the assigned mission.

Rommel underwent intensive mountain-warfare training in Austria. He then spent a quiet year in the Vosges Mountains in northeast France. Rommel managed to slip away on leave long enough to marry Lucie in Danzig on November 27, 1916, after which his battalion was assigned to the elite *Alpenkorps* (Alpine Corps) in Romania toward the end of the year. Romania had joined the Allied side in the war in August 1916, hoping to gain independence from Austro-Hungarian rule.

Two engagements in Romania added luster to Rommel's growing reputation. In January 1917, Rommel, now in command of an *Abteilung*, led his men in a successful night infiltration of the enemy-held village of Gagesti in freezing weather. After a brief firefight, Rommel and his men collected some 400 prisoners. The following August, after a short stint back in France, Rommel's battalion returned to Romania and participated in a two-week battle for possession of the Romanian-held Mount Cosna. Although struck by a bullet in his left arm—his third wound— Rommel led four companies through the woods in single file undetected, then attacked and captured the Romanian mountain stronghold.

In the fall and winter of 1917, Rommel reached the high point of his World War I career, fittingly enough, in the Julian Alps along the Austro-Italian frontier. Italy had entered the war on the side of the Allies in 1915, hoping to win back the Adriatic port of Trieste. The city had placed itself under the protection of the Habsburg (Austro-Hungarian) throne in 1382. Over several centuries, the Habsburgs gradually assimilated the outlet to the sea.

By the time Rommel arrived at the Italian border on September 26, 1917, eleven battles had already been fought along the Isonzo, the frontier river separating Italy and Austria (now Italy and Slovenia). A twelfth battle—the Battle of Caporetto (October 24–November 12, 1917)— was set to begin.

Fifty Italian infantry divisions, supported by thousands of guns (cannons), had crossed the middle reaches of the Isonzo. The heavily outnumbered Austrians appealed to the Germans for help. Responding to the Austrian plea, the German high command speedily united seven German and eight Austrian divisions to create the Fourteenth Army under General of Infantry Otto von Below and sent it to the Isonzo front. Rommel viewed the impending battle—sometimes called the Twelfth Battle of the Isonzo—as a chance to earn the prized *Pour le Mérite*. The medal for meritorious conduct in combat was the German equivalent to the British Victoria Cross

In November 1917, when German troops came to the aid of Austrian forces along the Italian border, Rommel again used his wits to outflank his enemy and result in the surrender of 1,500 Italian soldiers. Rommel believed this victory would garner him a coveted medal (the *Pour le Mérite*), but he was overlooked.

or the American Medal of Honor. Twice he would experience bitter disappointment in his quest for the medal.

General von Below's strategy—that is, his plan for the entire operation—was to penetrate the main Italian defense line south of the Isonzo. The river itself formed a part of the forward Italian defense line. An intermediate line stood behind it, followed by the main line in the high mountain ridges behind the intermediate line. To carry out Below's plan, his army would have to surmount the line's towering high points—Monte (Mount) Cragonza, Monte Kuk, Monte Matajur, the Kolovrat Ridge, Hill 1114, and others. Tens of thousands of Italian troops commanded these treacherous high points, well ensconced in formidable gun positions. The *Pour le Mérite*, it seemed, would not come easy.

The Württemberg Mountain Battalion was again attached to the Alpine Corps and was assigned to attack in the center of the Italian positions, toward Monte Matajur. On the first day, it was to protect the right flank of a Bavarian regiment that was to lead the attack. Thereafter, it would follow behind the advancing Bavarians. Given three mountain companies and a machine-gun company (called, as always, "The Rommel Detachment"), Rommel wanted no part of bringing up the rear. He persuaded his superior, battalion commander Major Theodor Sprösser, to allow him to move off to the right and mount an independent attack on the enemy.

Sprösser's report of the battle, written later, describes the menacing obstacles his battalion faced. "Like fortresses,"

Pour le Mérite

The distinguished Prussian *Orden Pour le Mérite* (Order for Merit) – often shortened to *Pour le Mérite* and more popularly known as the "Blue Max" – was established on June 6, 1740, by Frederick II ("Frederick the Great") of Prussia. It was awarded for both civil and military distinguished service. Two Prussian colonels and a state minister became the first recipients of the award at the end of June 1740. By the end of the decade, some 300 of the medals had been awarded. In 1810, qualifications for earning the *Pour le Mérite* changed and it was reserved for only those who demonstrated outstanding bravery or military achievement against an enemy in the field.

The decoration was formed in the shape of a Maltese Cross in blue enamel and edged in gold. The cross's upper arm bore a gold "F" (for Frederick) surmounted by a gold crown. Its left, right, and lower arms respectively displayed in gold letters the inscriptions "Pour," "le Mé," and "rite." A gold Prussian eagle nestled in each of the four "vees" formed by the arms of the cross. Holders of the *Pour le Mérite* wore the medal around the neck hung on a black ribbon with white stripes interwoven with silver toward each edge.

During the Franco-Prussian War (1870–1871) and the First World War I (1914–1918), the *Pour le Mérite* was Germany's highest award for gallantry in action. After the defeat of Germany in 1918, the award was discontinued.

he wrote, "the strongly built gun positions . . . look out over us. They are manned by hard-bitten machine-gunners, and bar our further advance to south and west."[19]

The battleground was made up of towering mountains, deep ravines, sheer cliffs, swirling mists, and raging rivers. That night, Rommel reconnoitered the enemy defenses and found a gap in the Italian lines. At 2:00 A.M. on October 24, a thousand German guns played overture to the German attack, blasting the enemy fortifications with high-explosive and gas projectiles. That morning, Rommel led his detachment through the gap. Three hours later, he stormed Monte Kuk. The Italians panicked to find Germans to their rear, and 40 officers and 1,500 men surrendered to Rommel's detachment.

Rommel felt that he warranted the *Pour le Mérite* for this accomplishment, but the medal that day went to a Bavarian lieutenant for capturing Hill 1114, the key to the entire Kolovrat Ridge. Rommel was outraged at being overlooked for the award, but there would be more opportunities for him to distinguish himself. General von Below had personally promised the medal to the first German officer to stand on the summit of Monte Matajur, the loftiest Italian strongpoint at 5,400 feet. Not to be denied, Rommel pressed on toward Matajur. Major Sprösser later reported:

> There is an Italian with a machine-gun sitting behind virtually every rock, and all the appearances are that the enemy has no intention of giving up Monte Mataiur [Matajur] so easily. Although their strength is almost at an end after fifty-three hours of continual full-pack march and battle, Rommel's *Abteilung* crawls in to close quarters. After a hail of machine-gun fire, which has a murderous splinter effect among the rocks, the enemy tries to escape into a ravine.[20]

The Italians did not escape. By 11:30 A.M., the last of another 1,200 men had surrendered to Rommel. Ten minutes later, Rommel stood atop Matajur's summit and fired off one white and three green flares to proclaim his triumph. Surely, the *Pour le Mérite* would now be his. But no, the medal went to a Silesian commander whose company had captured another summit that was misidentified as Matajur. Rommel was furious, but Sprösser advised him not to pursue the matter. The disappointment failed to flag Rommel's fighting zeal.

With his detachment at the head of the Württemberg Mountain Battalion, which, in turn, was spearheading the entire Fourteenth Army, Rommel pursued the retreating Italians southward. He led his troops to the limit of their endurance through fresh snowfalls and over precipitous cliff faces, reaching the Tagliamento River on November 4. His tactics of rapid pursuit, bravado, bluff, and surprise attack would later distinguish his actions as a tank commander.

On November 9, Rommel reached the Piave River. At dusk, with six men, he swam the river's icy waters and positioned his men around the town of Longarone — the hub of the entire Italian mountain defense system. Rommel ordered his handful of men to commence firing on the town from their widely dispersed locations. After this bluffed show of force, Rommel walked boldly into the village where he demanded and received the surrender of its garrison.

During his ruthless advance — through maneuver and sheer audacity — Rommel captured, in total, some 150 officers, 9,000 enlisted men, and 81 guns. For this remarkable effort, he was promoted to *Hauptmann* (captain) and was finally awarded the *Pour le Mérite*. He wore the distinctive cross around his neck on a ribbon. Years later, Rommel told an old school friend, "You can't imagine how jealous the officers are of my Pour le Mérite. There's no spirit of comradeship at all."[21] But he did not mind. The medal more than made up for any lack of camaraderie.

His victory at Longarone ended Rommel's combat activities in World War I. After taking another leave, he returned to duty and was assigned to staff duty for the rest of the war. By then, he had already established himself as a brilliant young officer. Moreover, he had been thrice wounded and decorated with the Iron Cross, First and Second Classes, and the *Pour le Mérite*—not too bad for a junior officer who had once been appraised no better than "a useful soldier."

3

Knight's Cross

On December 21, 1918, Rommel, after having served with
other units during the war, rejoined the 124th Württemberg
Infantry Regiment. He returned to a Germany that was suffering
in the throes of postwar economic chaos and collective confusion
of national spirit. A series of Allied victories on the battlefield
and years of deprivation brought on by an Allied blockade had
weakened the will of the German people to continue fighting.
The harsh surrender terms imposed on Germany by the Allies in
the Treaty of Versailles further worsened the economic, social,
and political upheaval that gripped Germany in the war's after-
math. But Rommel's career was virtually unaffected by the
national unrest.

The Treaty of Versailles, which ended World War I, also imposed stiff penalties and regulations on Germany—among them, that the German army never exceed 100,000 men. Surviving these severe cutbacks, Rommel helped to rebuild Germany's military might.

The Treaty of Versailles mandated that after March 31, 1920, the German Army "must not exceed 100,000 men, including officers and establishment of depots. . . . The total effective strength of officers . . . must not exceed 4,000."[22] The Allies intended to limit the Germans to a military force no larger than was necessary for the maintenance of internal order. Contrary to Allied intentions, however, this small force of seasoned professional soldiers effectively provided the Germans with the nucleus of a much larger army that would come of age in a much greater future war.

Rommel—holder of the *Pour le Mérite* and a solid reputation as a regimental commander—represented exactly the kind of career officer needed to rebuild Germany's broken army. He handily survived the army's reduction to 4,000 officers and remained in the service as one of its most promising junior commanders.

Over the next two years, the future field marshal served with his old regiment in Weingarten, commanded an internal security company in Friedrichshafen, and served a year in a training regiment in Schwäbisch Gemund. On October 1, 1920, he took command of a rifle company in the Thirteenth Infantry Regiment in nearby Stuttgart. He spent the next nine years mastering the army's training and administrative practices.

These were good years for the Rommels, who enjoyed living in Stuttgart. They rode, skied, traveled, and also found time to become parents. Lucie presented her life's partner with a son on Christmas Eve 1928. Rommel called the boy Manfred, a clear indication of a father's high aspirations for his son. (Germany's greatest flying ace of World War I bore the same first name — Manfred von Richthofen, the Red Baron.) Rommel's happiest experiences came always in the company of his beloved wife and son.

In September 1929, Rommel's battalion commander lauded his "very great military gifts" and went on to note that he "has already demonstrated in the war that he is an exemplary combat commander" and that he "has shown very good results in training and drilling his company;" the commander concluded that there "is more to this officer than meets the eye"[23] and noted that Rommel might make a good military instructor. A month later, Rommel was assigned to the Infantry School at Dresden.

During his four-year tenure at Dresden, Rommel authored a book called *Infantry Attacks*. He based it on personal observations and his own experiences in World War I. The published book earned him a tidy profit. More important, in terms of his career, the book would later draw him to the favorable attention of Adolf Hitler, who was appointed Germany's chancellor (chief of state) on January 30, 1933.

Hitler had risen to the heights of power on vows to purge Germany of Jews and Communists, rebuild the strength of its armed forces, cast off the shackles of Versailles, and conquer "by the sword" the land it needed to provide more "living space"[24] (*Lebensraum*) for German citizens. With his pledge to rebuild Germany's armed forces, Hitler won the admiration and loyalty of most German career military men, including, at first, Rommel. But Rommel had strong reservations about some of the Nazis surrounding the Führer.

While serving in various assignments with devotion and diligence, promotions began to come rapidly for Rommel. On October 10, 1933, he was promoted to major and appointed commander of the Third Battalion, Seventeenth Infantry Regiment, a mountain unit undergoing training at Goslar in the Harz Mountains. Two years later, on October 15, 1935, he was elevated to *Oberstleutnant* (lieutenant colonel) and posted to the War College in Potsdam as an instructor. On November 9, 1938, as a full colonel (*Oberst*), he moved on to his next assignment as director of the War College at Wiener Neustadt.

During Rommel's term at Wiener Neustadt, Hitler called him away from time to time on temporary duty as the chief of the Führer's personal security battalion. Rommel accompanied Hitler during Germany's takeover of Czechoslovakia's Sudetenland in October 1938 and in Prague during its seizure of Czechoslovakia itself on March 19, 1939. Although Rommel never joined the Nazi Party, he enthusiastically supported Hitler in the early days. He also served as an instructor to the Hitler *Jugend* (Youth)—the male branch of the German youth movement, which was considered a *Gliederung* (limb) of the Nazi Party.

On August 23, 1939, Rommel was elevated to *General-major* (brigadier general) and transferred to Hitler's headquarters, where he again assumed responsibility for the Führer's safety. Hitler had ordered Rommel's promotion backdated to June 1, which was a sign that Rommel was gaining favor with the Führer. When Hitler launched his *Blitzkrieg* (lightning war) against Poland nine days later, Rommel was well positioned to see the campaign from the top. Although he played no active part in the campaign that overwhelmed Poland in four weeks, Rommel carefully observed the new techniques of warfare that featured rapid mechanized thrusts deep into enemy territory and emphasized close cooperation between air and ground forces.

In a letter to Lucie on September 23, with the campaign against Poland nearing its end, Rommel wrote: "The Führer's in a relaxed mood. We eat at his table twice a day now—yesterday evening I was allowed to sit next to him. Soldiers are worth something again." [25] Rommel, perhaps eager to demonstrate again his own worth as a soldier, would soon use his close ties with Hitler to arrange a transfer to a combat command.

Hitler's unprovoked attack on Poland marked the start of World War II. Great Britain and France immediately declared war on Germany and became known as the Allies, or Allied Powers. Germany had allied itself with Italy and Japan to form the Axis, or Axis Powers. Italy remained neutral until joining Germany in the war in June 1940. Japan joined Germany and Italy by launching a surprise attack on the U.S. naval base at Pearl Harbor on December 7, 1941, which, in turn, brought the United States into the war on the side of the Allies.

After the fall of Poland on September 27, 1939, Rommel returned to Berlin, where he continued his duties as Hitler's protector. With a war on, however,

Hitler's lightning-quick attack on Poland yielded a Germany victory in only four weeks. This photograph shows Hitler and his officers talking to Polish-Germans after the invasion. Although Rommel was not part of this *Blitzkrieg*, he took the opportunity to build his strategic military expertise.

Rommel ached for a combat assignment. Hitler—who had served as a corporal in World War I—had by then become quite fond of Rommel, as much for his modest beginnings as for his outstanding military record. Empathizing with Rommel's desire for a combat command, Hitler asked, "What do you want?"[26]

Replying without a second thought, Rommel asked for "command of a Panzer [tank] Division."[27] Hitler granted his request and posted him to Godesberg on the Rhine, where Rommel took command of the Seventh Panzer Division on February 15, 1940.

Rommel joined the Seventh Panzers during the so-called "Phony War"—a six-month period after the German conquest of Poland (October 1939–March 1940), during which neither the Allies nor the Germans undertook any action. Rommel took advantage of the lull to familiarize himself with the men, weapons, and tactics—the art of placing or maneuvering forces skillfully in battle—of his new command, particularly its tanks.

The Seventh Panzer Division consisted of a Panzer regiment (the Twenty-Fifth) of three battalions with a total of 218 tanks; an armored reconnaissance battalion (the Thirty-Seventh) equipped with three-axle armored cars mounted with a 38-mm gun; two rifle regiments,

Panzers!

With the invasion of Poland on September 1, 1939, Germany introduced a new form of warfare—the *Blitzkrieg* (lightning war). This new warfare featured a surprise offensive conducted with great speed and force by massed air and mechanized forces in close coordination. Most battle buffs credit General Heinz Guderian as being "the father of *Blitzkrieg*." *Panzers* (tanks) spearheaded the German ground offensive in Poland to shock the world with Guderian's new concept of lightning warfare.

Major General Erwin Rommel joined the ranks of famous tank commanders at the head of the Seventh Panzer Division during its race across France in the spring of 1940. Although more than half of his tanks were of Czech manufacture and lightly armored, his division relied heavily on the superior German-built Panzer IIIs and IVs.

The Panzer III was a medium tank that provided the bulk of the panzer divisions' strength early in the war. Its specifications varied according to its variants (at least 20) but generally speaking, the Panzer III was roughly 18 feet long, 10 feet wide, and 9 feet tall. Armed with a 37-mm gun and two 7.92-mm machine guns, it weighed about 22 tons, bore 30-mm armor plating, and carried a crew of five. Its Maybach HL120TRM engine powered it to speeds of 25 (or more) miles an hour over a range of 101 miles.

The Panzer IV—also a medium tank—was slightly larger than its predecessor, its main gun was upgraded to 75-mm, and its range was extended to 125 miles.

each containing three battalions; a motorcycle battalion; and an engineer battalion. Its divisional artillery support comprised one field regiment (9 batteries, 36 guns) and an antitank battalion with 75 antitank guns. More than half of the division's tanks were of Czech manufacture and lightly armored; the rest consisted of superlative German-built Panzer IIIs and IVs.

The Panzers were 22-ton behemoths that stood nine feet tall and housed a crew of five. Powered by a 320-horsepower (hp) Maybach gasoline engine, the Panzers could attain a top speed of about 25 miles per hour (mph). Rommel would soon give them a chance to show what they could do.

In about three months of inactivity, Rommel made himself known to all of the men in his division and became personally acquainted with all of his officers. He also found time to direct intensive training exercises to develop his own theories on tank tactics. Rommel drew heavily on the writings of leading German tank theorist General Heinz Guderian and on his own observations during the campaign in Poland. Guderian was a pioneer in tank warfare and the commander of the German Fourth Army's XIX Corps in Poland. Military historians often refer to him as "the father of *Blitzkrieg*."[28] In May 1940, Rommel, a newcomer to tanks, stood ready to blaze new tank trails.

On May 10, Hitler launched his *Sichelschnitt* (Sickle Cut) offensive, the long-awaited German invasion of Western Europe. The German strategy—known as Plan Yellow—called for an invasion of Holland and Belgium to draw the British Expeditionary Force (BEF) and much of the French strength northward. Once the Allies moved to the north, the bulk of the German armor was then to break through the weakly defended Ardennes sector, cross the Meuse River, and cut a swath across northern France to the English Channel. In effect, this "sickle cut" to the Channel would form a pocket in which to trap the Allied forces in the north. The role of Rommel's Panzers in this operation was to form the *Schwerpunkt*—the cutting edge of the sickle—in the drive through France.

In true *Blitzkrieg* fashion, Rommel, leading from the front of his division, raced at maximum speeds across the northern part of Luxembourg without resistance and crossed into Belgium about 30 miles south of Liège, sweeping aside slight opposition. In his later account of these first encounters, Rommel wrote: "Experience in this early fighting showed that in tank attacks especially, the action of opening fire immediately into the area which the enemy is believed to be holding, instead of waiting until several of one's own tanks have been hit, usually decides the issue."[29] Rommel and his Panzers decided a lot of such issues this way on their race to the sea.

Rommel clanked across the Ourthe River on the morning of May 11, cleared away French defenders, and rumbled on to the Meuse River near Dinant, arriving on the afternoon of May 12. He experienced his first real difficulties at the Meuse when his attempted crossing came under heavy fire from French defenders who expected to hold back the German advance at the river for at least a week. But through skillful generalship and personal example, Rommel—who appeared to be everywhere at once—established a bridgehead on the west side of the river.

On one occasion, at the site of a pontoon bridge, Rommel pitched in with a crew of sappers (engineers) and hauled beams of timbers into waist-deep water to move the work along. "I'll give you a hand,"[30] he said, and labored with his men until the job was done. He then directed his tanks across the river, and their guns

In May 1940, Rommel led his heavily armored yet fast-moving Panzer tanks through Luxembourg and into Belgium as part of Hitler's "Sickle Cut" plan. Again, Rommel had successfully used speed and decisiveness to surprise his enemy.

soon silenced those of the enemy. Word of Rommel's brand of leadership traveled rapidly throughout the ranks, and his men came to know quickly that he was a special kind of commander.

After repulsing a French counterattack, Rommel's Panzers turned southwest toward Philippeville on May 14, having overcome French expectations of a week's delay at the Meuse in only two days. Rommel pressed his attack deep into enemy territory in the only style he knew—from the front, with maximum speed and unsurpassed audacity, his every move calculated to amaze, confuse, and eventually paralyze his adversaries.

At least twice, he was almost killed on his tank. Many of his men began to ask, "Is Rommel immune?"[31]

One by one, Rommel rolled over his objectives en route to the Channel, breezing through a barely formed French stop-line (line of resistance) east of Philippeville on May 15, then penetrating the Maginot Line extension near Sivry the next night. (The Maginot Line, named for its principal creator, was an ultramodern defensive barrier along the French-German frontier, complete with concrete fortifications, living quarters, supply store-houses, and underground rail lines.) "Ahead of us," Rommel wrote later, recapturing the view from his tank's turret, "the flat countryside unfurled in the moon's wan light. We were through—through the Maginot Line."[32] His Panzers now drove deep into France.

Along the main east–west road, moving almost 50 miles in two days, Rommel captured Avesnes, Landrecies, and Le Cateau on May 17, then pushed on west to seize Cambrai on May 19. He reached Arras on May 20 but took three days to capture it. On May 21, heavily armored British Matilda Mark II tanks bore down on his Panzers. The Matildas were immune to the standard 37-mm shell, so Rommel brought his big 88-mm guns to bear on them.

"With the enemy tanks so dangerously close, only rapid fire from every gun could save the situation," Rommel wrote later. "We ran from gun to gun. I brushed aside the gun commanders' objections that the range was too great."[33] His dynamic leadership gave heart to his men and inspired them to stand fast in their worst encounter of the campaign.

Rommel's advance rolled on, turning northeasterly toward Lille on May 26. With Lille besieged by Rommel's Panzers, Hitler summoned Rommel to a conference on June 2. "Rommel, we were very worried about you during the attack,"[34] Hitler told him. At the secret meeting, Hitler announced plans for a new offensive set to begin on June 5. France was to be given the *coup de grâce* (death blow). "It will be easy to find a basis for peace with Britain," the Führer said, "but France must be smashed into the ground, and then she must pay the bill."[35]

Turning south, the German Army proceeded to finish off the already weakened French over the next three weeks. Crossing the Somme River between Abbeville and Amiens and advancing southward to the Seine River at breakneck speeds, Rommel added to his string of victories at Elbeuf on June 10. He then turned his Panzers to the northwest and reached the coast between Fécamp and St.-Valéry-en-Caux, where he trapped thousands of British and French troops attempting to flee across the Channel. One French general told Rommel frankly upon surrendering to him, "You are too rapid for us."[36]

Rommel next set his eyes on Cherbourg. Resuming his advance to the south and west, he returned to the Seine, then rolled through Evreux, Falaise, and Flers, before turning north to the port of La Haye du Puit. Traveling at speeds of 20 to 30 miles an hour, Rommel's tanks covered 200 miles in two days. In a single day, he advanced 150 miles, a record at the time. He churned into Cherbourg on June 17. Thirty thousand of his enemies surrendered to him two days later, which was nothing new to Rommel.

During the Battle of France, Rommel and his Panzers captured the awesome sum of almost 100,000 prisoners and more than 450 enemy tanks. While doing so, his losses totaled 682 dead, 1,646 wounded, and 296 missing. He lost 42 tanks. Rommel's campaign added an astounding chapter to the book of *Blitzkrieg* and scribed his name on the roll of great tank commanders.

The Panzer was, in its time, a marvel of military engineering. Although each tank weighed 22 tons, it was powered by a 320-horsepower engine, allowing for surprisingly swift maneuvers.

Because of Rommel's swift and unexpected appearances—time and time again across the battlefront—correspondents, both friendly and hostile, began referring to him as the "Knight of the Apocalypse."[37] Similarly, the surprise thrusts of his Seventh Panzer Division in unpredictable locales and situations earned for it, in the journalistic idiom, the sobriquet of *"Gespensterdivision,"* or "Ghost Division."[38]

During the six weeks of Rommel's personal *Blitzkrieg* in France, he was wounded once and nearly captured, was almost killed at least twice, and was decorated three times. He earned a clasp to his Iron Cross (Second Class) for his actions on May 13, and another to his Iron Cross

(First Class) for his deeds on May 15. And for his division's victories over the next two days, he received the Knight's Cross of the Iron Cross, the highest degree of the Iron Cross (which could be augmented further with oak leaves, swords, and diamonds). The citation extolled the divisional commander's personal valor "regardless of danger" during victories "of decisive significance for the whole operation."[39]

4

The Fox and the Hound

After seizing Cherbourg on June 17, 1940, Rommel swept southward to Rennes and continued on to the Spanish frontier, before returning to the Bordeaux area to assume occupation duties. Despite his phenomenal leadership and performance in France, he had to wait until January 1941 for promotion to *generalleutnant* (lieutenant general; equivalent to U.S. major general). Meanwhile, over the remainder of 1940, his future was evolving in the echelons of high command.

Following Hitler's whirlwind campaign in France and the evacuation of Allied troops from the Continent, primarily at Dunkirk (May 26–June 3, 1940), he launched an air offensive on England. Now known as the Battle of Britain, it was aimed at

These British Royal Air Force patrol planes are in flight over an unknown location in France just prior to the start of the Battle of Britain.

preparing the island nation for invasion. Thanks to the Royal Air Force (RAF) and its victory over the *Luftwaffe*, however, Hitler was forced to abandon his plans for invading England ("Operation Sea Lion") in September 1940. That same month, Italian dictator Benito Mussolini— who had joined Hitler's assault on France in June (after a German victory had been assured)—opened a new theater of operations in North Africa.

Mussolini sent his army of a half-million strong in Libya against a British force of 30,000 men in Egypt, in an apparent effort to seize the Suez Canal. After some initial, inconclusive successes, the Italians stopped at Sidi Barani to await supplies. In October 1940, Mussolini extended his offensive operations to Greece and met unexpectedly fierce resistance. Starting on December 9, a

British counteroffensive by General Sir Archibald Wavell's Army of the Nile ousted the Italian invaders from Egypt and shoved them out of Cyrenaica, the eastern half of Libya. Mussolini appealed to Hitler for help.

In January 1941, Hitler responded to his fellow dictator's request by sending Luftwaffe elements to Italy to provide cover for Italian ground forces and protection for Axis shipping in the Mediterranean. A month later, he appointed Rommel to command the newly forming *Deutsches Afrika Korps* (or DAK, the German Africa Corps). "In view of the highly critical situation with our Italian allies," Rommel noted later, "two German divisions—one light and one panzer—were to be sent to Libya to their help."[40]

Hitler, as he said later, had picked Rommel for the job "because he knows how to *inspire* his troops," a quality that he considered "absolutely essential for a commander of a force that has to fight under particularly arduous climatic conditions."[41]

In his new assignment, Rommel would face harsh terrain; sandstorms; extreme temperature variations; vast distances; deficient food for his troops; ongoing shortages of ammunition, fuel, and other essentials; numerically inferior forces; and a wealth of other difficulties. Despite such adversities, he would repeatedly demonstrate his flair for generating the unpredictable, while broadening his battlefield perspective from a tactical outlook to a strategic overview.

The German Fifth Light Division began moving to Libya in mid-February, with its movement scheduled for completion by mid-April. It was to be joined by the Fifteenth Panzer Division in its entirety by the end of May. Rommel flew into Tripoli, the capital of Libya, on February 12, 1941. In Libya, he was to operate under high-level Italian supervision with several Italian armored divisions under him. Rommel's mission, which was primarily defensive, was to prevent the expulsion of the Italians from North Africa.

Upon Rommel's arrival in Libya, the strategic situation looked bleak. In less than two months, the British offensive had advanced nearly 400 miles westward from Egypt, seizing Tobruk, Derna, Benghazi, the capital of Cyrenaica, and El Agheila, the gateway to Tripolitania (a former Italian province in northwest Libya). Wavell's offensive resulted in the capture of about 130,000 Italian troops, 1,300 guns, and 400 tanks.

Wavell, the British commander in chief of the Middle East, might very well have continued his drive and seized Tripoli, but the British government, at the urging of Prime Minister Winston Churchill, decided to intervene in Greece. Their decision diverted a corps from Wavell's forces and compelled him to halt his drive. The Italians, unaware of this troop diversion, pleaded with Rommel to save Tripoli.

On the afternoon of his arrival in Tripoli, Rommel took off again in a twin-engine Heinkel 111 to "get to know the country." [42] He learned that, except for the Via Balbia, the Italian-built highway that rimmed the Mediterranean, the land lacked any readily distinguishable features as it rose from the narrow coastal plain to the dun-colored boulder-strewn plateau inland. Occasionally, a patch of green appeared where farmers had installed irrigation systems. Otherwise, as Rommel wrote later, the macadam road "stretched away like a black thread through the desolate landscape, in which neither tree nor bush could be seen as far as the eye could reach."[43] In such bleakness, this portion of the great desert called Sahara extended eastward for more than 1,200 miles into Egypt.

From the air, of course, Rommel could not feel the blazing desert heat that often exceeded 120°F, or feel the bite of wind-driven sand on flesh, or discern the swarms of black flies and sand fleas and the scattered prickly bushes called camel thorns that gave a semblance of life to the barren wasteland. These unpleasantries—and more—he was soon to experience as a way of life for months at a time. First, however, with the situation in Libya temporarily stabilized, Rommel journeyed to Hitler's headquarters on March 19 to receive Oak Leaves to the Knight's Cross for his actions in France, and to propose a plan for a new offensive in North Africa.

In Germany, Rommel abruptly learned the limits of his new assignment. Hitler told him that he had no intention of striking a decisive blow in North Africa any time soon. As a consequence, Rommel could expect no reinforcements. The *Oberkommando der Wehrmacht*, or OKW (High Command of the Armed Forces), directed Rommel to hold his defensive line in Libya until the arrival of the Fifteenth Panzer Division in late May, after which he could engage in limited offensive action. If successful, however, he was to advance no farther than Benghazi under any circumstances.

Hitler and the OKW were too preoccupied with the fighting in Greece and plans to invade Russia (in June 1941) to lend support for a full-scale offensive in North Africa. But Rommel was by nature offensive-minded. He held a grand vision of how the desert war should be fought. He viewed the desert as a vast sea of sand and thus conducive to the employment of naval tactics using tanks instead of ships. Rommel returned to Tripoli, eager to test his theories.

He struck on March 31. With only a partially formed corps, Rommel launched a reconnaissance in force—an aggressive patrol—that soon turned into an impromptu, full-fledged offensive against the British. He first recaptured Mersa el Brega. Then, after a swift and decisive tank battle, Rommel drove the British out of Agedabia on April 2, thus achieving the goals set by the OKW for June. "I decided to stay on the heels of the retreating enemy,"

After Mussolini's Italian troops met stiff resistance in Libya and Egypt, Hitler appointed Rommel commander of the German Africa Corps. Although ordered to simply defend Axis positions, Rommel soon chose to take the offensive, recapturing key desert cities from the British.

he wrote later, "and make a bid to seize the whole of Cyrenaica at one stroke." [44]

Rommel pressed on eastward, forcing the British to abandon El Agheila and to surrender Benghazi. By the end of April, all of Cyrenaica—except Tobruk, which he invested (besieged)—belonged to Rommel and his *Afrika Korps*. At the Egyptian frontier, he ran out of gas and was forced to stop. Rommel's actions had far exceeded his orders, but, as he explained in a letter to Lucie, "I took the risk against all orders and instructions because the opportunity seemed favorable." [45] His risk had paid off, catching the British by complete surprise.

Unknown to Rommel, the British had learned through "Ultra" intercepts that the DAK was not supposed to reach full strength in North Africa until June; hence, they did not expect an attack before then. ("Ultra" was the British security classification for the highly secret intelligence produced by the interception and deciphering of German and Italian coded messages sent by radio and other means.) But Rommel outfoxed them. In so doing, he regained the territory lost by the Italians, captured two British generals, and earned the nickname of the "Desert Fox" for his cunning and audacity. Rommel and his sobriquet will likely remain forever linked.

Following Rommel's successes in April, Winston Churchill pressured Wavell to destroy "Rommel's audacious force."[46] Wavell launched "Operation Battleaxe" in June, a three-pronged attack intended to destroy Rommel's forces in the Sollum-Halfaya area, relieve Tobruk, and drive the Axis forces as far west as possible.

Wavell's counterattack failed. In fairness to Wavell, British forces were fighting not only in North Africa but also in Greece, Syria, and elsewhere in Africa and they were accordingly stretched thin. Wavell had to make do with fewer troops, many of whom were inexperienced. Upon hearing of Wavell's failure, Churchill lamented, "Rommel has torn the new-won laurels from Wavell's brow and thrown them in the sand."[47] Churchill replaced Wavell with General Sir Claude J.A. Auchinleck in June.

The same battle that plunged Wavell's military career into sharp decline also sent Rommel's martial fortunes soaring. Rommel's quick victories in the Sahara stunned both the Allies and Rommel's own superiors. Auchinleck's first order of business was to exhort his subordinates not to think of Rommel as either a magician or a demon but rather as just an ordinary German general. "We speak too much of our friend Rommel,"[48] he told them. Auchinleck misspoke. Rommel was many things, but none of them ordinary.

On June 22, 1941, Hitler unleashed "Operation Barbarossa," the invasion of the Soviet Union. The Führer, confident of a victory against the Soviets, now fantasized about a converging German offensive against British positions in the Middle East. He planned to attack from Libya into Egypt, and from Bulgaria through Turkey and the soon-to-be-conquered Caucasus.

The Libyan arm of the projected offensive would belong to Rommel, whose forces had grown into the *Panzergruppe Afrika*, comprising the DAK, two Italian armored divisions, and four Italian infantry divisions. But the Soviets proved far tougher than Hitler had anticipated. Rommel spent the summer and most of the autumn of 1941 waiting in vain for the substantial reinforcements, supplies, and matériel that he would need to conduct his desert offensive. While Hitler's eastern armies drove toward Moscow, Auchinleck attacked Rommel on November 18.

Auchinleck's offensive—code-named "Operation Crusader"—was carried out by the newly formed British Eighth Army under Lieutenant General Sir Alan Cunningham, who was relieved in mid-operation by Major General Sir Neil N. Ritchie. The Eighth Army contained two corps, the Thirtieth and the Thirteenth. At first, Rommel did not believe that the British attack was a new offensive. He insisted that the British meant "only to harass us" and scoffed, "We must not lose our nerve."[49] But by month's end, the British forced Rommel, who was still dangerously low on supplies, to retreat.

Rommel elected to give ground in order to save his forces, and he began a gradual fighting withdrawal westward. In the swath of desolate territory between Tobruk and the Egyptian-Libyan border, two mechanized armies churned across the desert sands and fought a running battle of constant maneuver. Major Friedrich von Mellenthin,

At Tobruk, Libya, Rommel met harsher than expected resistance from Allied forces. British persistence and heavy Allied bombing forced Rommel to retreat, using his Panzers to wage a running battle across the desert. The fighting left the city of Tobruk in ruins.

Rommel's intelligence officer, would later describe the fighting this way:

> Never has a battle been fought at such an extreme pace and with such bewildering vicissitudes of fortune. More than a thousand tanks, supported by large numbers of aircraft and guns, were committed to a whirlwind battle fought on ground that allowed complete freedom of manoeuvre, and were handled by commanders who were prepared to throw in their last reserves to achieve victory. The situation changed so rapidly that it was difficult to keep track of the movements of one's own troops, let alone those of the enemy.[50]

The British drove Rommel out of Sidi Rezegh at the end of November. Rommel quit Benghazi around Christmas, and, continuing his fighting withdrawal a step at a time, arrived at his Mersa el Brega defensive line on January 12, 1942. Operation Crusader had cost Rommel some 38,000 killed, missing, and wounded, and about 340 tanks.

In December 1941, Hitler had sent Field Marshal Albert Kesselring and another Luftwaffe contingent to Italy.

Malta

In the North African desert campaigns in World War II, victory usually belonged to the side with the most gasoline. The desert war literally ran on gasoline – and like almost all other commodities, gasoline had to be transported over vast distances and at great costs. Because the main British supply route to North Africa extended 3,000 miles around the Cape of Good Hope (compared to the Axis supply route across the Mediterranean of only 300 miles), distances would appear to have favored Rommel. Throughout much of the desert war, however, British air and naval forces – based on the tiny island of Malta and tipped off to Axis supply movements by Ultra intercepts – negated Rommel's advantage.

Malta, located only 60 miles from Sicily, constituted Britain's only military base in the central Mediterranean. Following Italy's entry into the war in June 1940, the island became the only possible springboard for offensive operations against Axis supply routes to North Africa. In 1941, after Rommel's First Cyrenaican Campaign (March 31 – April 12), Hitler and Mussolini agreed that British air and naval bases on Malta needed to be destroyed and the island taken before Rommel could advance across Egypt. Churchill and his high command agreed on the need to hold the island at all costs.

The Luftwaffe struck Malta with a fury, flying 169 bombing raids against it in December 1941, and another 262 raids the next month. Britain expended enormous costs in men and matériel to defend and resupply the island. But the situation became desperate and Axis supplies began to slip through to North Africa. New supplies enabled Rommel to resume his offensive in January 1942 and drive all the way to the Gazala Line. Malta endured everything the Axis could send its way and kept on fighting.

Under Kesselring's direction, the Luftwaffe pummeled British air and naval bases on the island of Malta and seized control of the skies over the central Mediterranean. Reinforcements and supplies for Rommel at last began pouring into Tripoli on January 5, 1942. His command now expanded into *Panzerarmee Afrika*, consisting of all German units—the DAK (Fifteenth and Twenty-First Panzer Divisions) and the Ninetieth Light Division—and all Italian forces.

On the night of January 21, 1942, Rommel launched another wholly unexpected offensive and advanced 30 miles to El Agheila. Just as in March of the previous year, inexperienced British troops, directed by a clumsy command structure, progressively fell away before his surprise attack. His reconnaissance in force again quickly elevated into a full-scale offensive. Rommel pressed on to Benghazi a week later, and thence to Derna. The British finally dug in along the "Gazala Line"—a zone of minefields that extended southward from the Mediterranean to Bir Hackeim and the war of maneuver stabilized again. But Rommel's sudden push to regain lost territory added immensely to his growing reputation as the Desert Fox. The Führer awarded him the Swords to the Oak Leaves of the Knight's Cross and promoted him to *Generaloberst* (colonel general).

For the next four months, both sides remained inactive to ponder plans for future offensive actions. Churchill urged Auchinleck to attack again as soon as possible, but the Middle East commander wanted to delay until he could build up a force of overwhelming superiority. Finally, upon direct orders from London, Auchinleck targeted a date in early June to resume the British offensive. Rommel again struck first.

On the night of May 26–27, Rommel led his armor—tanks and half-tracked vehicles—around the Eighth Army's left (south) flank and attacked toward the sea and its rear. Rommel's armor drove to within 20 miles of the sea when it met unexpected opposition from recently acquired U.S.-built General Grant tanks, which had better guns than those of comparable British tanks. A savage two-week battle ensued.

"Nowhere in Africa was I given a stiffer fight,"[51] Rommel remarked later. But his *Panzerarmee* finally succeeded in driving British and Free French forces from the Bir Hackeim redoubt (fortification) on June 10–11. (The Free French were French patriots who fought on after the fall of France under General Charles de Gaulle.) Rommel pushed on to the long-besieged port of Tobruk, battling and overrunning British tanks positioned at a locale south of the port dubbed "Knightsbridge" by the British.

By June 14, the British were in full retreat toward Egypt. Rommel arrived at Tobruk four days later and surrounded the city. "To each one of us, Tobruk was a symbol of British resistance," Rommel said, "and we are now going to finish with it for good."[52] Rommel began his attack at 5:20 A.M. on June 20, and the British garrison surrendered the next morning.

Rommel's latest offensive exacted a heavy toll from the British. Their defeat at the Gazala Line cost them some 45,000 casualties; their loss at Tobruk, another 33,000. Axis losses, however, were equally heavy.

Rommel retired early that night, only to be awakened by one of his staff with news from Berlin: The Führer had promoted him. At age 49, Rommel was now the youngest *Generalfeldmarschall* (field marshal) in the German Army. The promotion pleased him but, as he later told Lucie, "I would much rather he had given me one more division."[53] Nevertheless, Rommel's elevation was well deserved and timely, for he had just reached the pinnacle of his career as a daring battlefield commander.

Thousands of miles away, Winston Churchill received

In August 1942, British General Bernard L. Montgomery (seen here) assumed control of the British Eighth Army in North Africa and stopped a desperate advance by Rommel's Panzers at Alam Halfa. The war in the desert had become a struggle between hound and fox.

word of Tobruk's fall while meeting with U.S. President Franklin D. Roosevelt in Washington, D.C. Churchill later called it a "shattering and grievous loss,"[54] but the loss encouraged Roosevelt to offer immediate help. As a result, the United States sent off some 300 Sherman tanks and 100 self-propelled guns to the Eighth Army in Egypt. Rommel would feel their impact later in the year during the Second Battle of El Alamein (or Alamein).

With Rommel standing at the Egyptian frontier, Hitler and his Italian allies decided to send Rommel on to the Suez Canal. Continuing his eastward drive, Rommel encountered a reinforced British Eighth Army between El Alamein and the Qattara Depression in Egypt in mid-July. Auchinleck launched a counterattack but could not break through Rommel's lines, and the two armies battled to a stalemate during the First Battle of El Alamein (July 1–27, 1942), about 65 miles west of Alexandria.

In August, London ordered two new figures to the desert theater: General Sir Harold L.R. Alexander, to relieve Auchinleck as British commander in chief, Middle East; and Lieutenant General Bernard L. Montgomery, to replace Ritchie as Eighth Army commander. The two new commanders met over tea at Shepheard's Hotel in Cairo, where Alexander issued a single order: "Go down to the desert and defeat Rommel."[55]

At the end of August, Rommel embarked on a last desperate attempt to reach the delta at Alexandria. But Montgomery, now at the head of a reinforced and revitalized Eighth Army, stopped the *Panzerarmee Afrika* at the Battle of Alam Halfa (August 31–September 2, 1942), southeast of El Alamein. By then, Rommel had extended his supply line about 1,000 miles from his main supply base at Tripoli. He would need considerable time to refurbish his forces. Montgomery learned of Rommel's supply problems through Ultra intercepts. With Egypt secure for the time being, Montgomery could concentrate on planning his own offensive to chase Rommel "right out of Africa."[56]

Montgomery, the hound, had caught the scent of his opponent and was now on the trail of Rommel, the fox.

5

Alamein

On September 22, 1942, with his *Panzerarmee Afrika* settled in along a line west of El Alamein and the fighting in Egypt at a standstill, Rommel left North Africa on a convalescent leave. His health had deteriorated enormously under the pressures of battle. He suffered from fainting spells, stomach and intestinal disorders, an enlarged liver, and high blood pressure—not to mention severe psychological stresses from his ongoing inability to guarantee adequate provisioning for his troops and his growing concern about an ultimate Axis victory. For the period of his projected absence, Rommel left his deputy, General Georg Stumme, in command of the *Panzerarmee Afrika*.

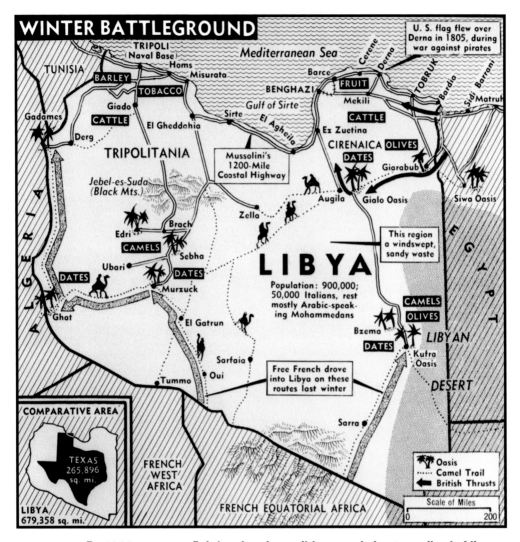

WINTER BATTLEGROUND

U. S. flag flew over Derna in 1805, during war against pirates

Mediterranean Sea

TRIPOLI (Naval Base)
Homs
TUNISIA
BARLEY
Misurata
TOBACCO
Giado
Gadames
CATTLE
El Gheddahia
Derg
Sirte
Gulf of Sirte
El Agheila
BENGHAZI
Barce
Cerene
Derna
TOBRUK
Bardia
Sidi Barrani
Matruh
FRUIT
Mekili
CATTLE
Ez Zuetina
CIRENAICA OLIVES
DATES
Giarabub

TRIPOLITANIA

Jebel-es-Suda (Black Mts.)

Mussolini's 1200-Mile Coastal Highway

Zella
Augila
Gialo Oasis
Siwa Oasis

Brach
Edri
CAMELS
Sebha
Ubari
DATES
Murzuck

This region a windswept, sandy waste

LIBYA

Population: 900,000; 50,000 Italians, rest mostly Arabic-speaking Mohammedans

Ghat

El Gatrun

Bzema
CAMELS
OLIVES
LIBYAN
DATES
Kufra Oasis

Sarfaia
Tummo
Oui

Free French drove into Libya on these routes last winter

DESERT

Sarra

COMPARATIVE AREA

TEXAS 265,896 sq. mi.

FRENCH WEST AFRICA

FRENCH EQUATORIAL AFRICA

LIBYA 679,358 sq. mi.

Oasis
Camel Trail
British Thrusts

Scale of Miles
0   200

ALGERIA

EGYPT

By 1942, constant fighting, harsh conditions, and short supplies in Libya began to take their toll on Rommel and his troops. This map shows the desert geography of Libya, once a rich farmland during the days of the Roman Empire, but now mostly desert.

During a stopover in Rome, Rommel met with Mussolini to discuss Axis strategy. "I left him no doubt that unless supplies were sent to us at least on the scale that I had demanded we should have to get out of

North Africa,"[57] Rommel wrote later. He suggested that unless adequate supplies were forthcoming it would be better to save the Axis troops in North Africa for the defense of Europe. But the Italian leader, as Rommel suspected, "did not realise the full gravity of the situation."[58] Mussolini felt that Rommel was overstating his problems and believed that the field marshal would find a way to win.

A few days later, Rommel aired his supply problems to Hitler, who promised an increase of supplies and weaponry in a few weeks. "Later," Rommel recounted, "it transpired that many of these promises had been given in a moment of over-optimism and on the basis of incorrect production figures."[59] During his meeting with the Führer, Hitler awarded Rommel the Oak Leaves with Swords and Diamonds to his Knight's Cross and presented him with his field marshal's baton. Still troubled by supply uncertainties, Rommel left with his spouse to recuperate at Semmering, a mountain resort near Vienna.

While convalescing, Rommel kept a close eye on the Axis submarine war against Allied shipping in the Atlantic Ocean (known as the Battle of the Atlantic). He knew all too well the enormous war production capacity of the United States. "I realised that there would be little hope left for us if the Americans and British succeeded in eliminating, or reducing to tolerable proportions, the U-boat [*Unterseeboot*, or submarine] threat to their convoys."[60] The Allies succeeded in doing precisely that a few months later. Nor was the news from North Africa particularly cheering to the field marshal.

The Royal Air Force and the British Eighth Army were growing stronger by the day, and his *Panzerarmee* was expecting a major British attack at any time, which did not bode well for the Axis forces. Rommel briefly assessed the situation this way:

> According to our estimates, the British had a two to one superiority in tanks. The figure included on our side the 300 Italian tanks, the fighting value of which was very small. We still had only a very few tanks armed with a 75-mm gun, whereas the British had many hundreds equipped with heavy guns [more than 500 armed with 75-mm guns]. Of our 210 German tanks only 30 or so were Panzer IVs; the majority were Panzer IIIs, which were the short-barrel type and hence very out of date. [Most of the Panzer IIIs were armed with short-barrel 50-mm guns.] As for the 300 Italian tanks . . . most of them were decrepit, and barely fit for action. Supplies were not being maintained at anything like the required level, so immense shortages existed in almost every field.[61]

Not surprisingly, Rommel found cause for concern. At 3:00 P.M. on October 24, his concern rose to alarm when he received a telephone call from his young aide, Lieutenant Alfred-Igemar Berndt, in Rome: "Montgomery's offensive has begun—last night! And General Stumme has vanished without a trace!"[62] *Afrika Korps* commander General Wilhelm Ritter von Thoma had assumed temporary command of the *Panzerarmee*. (Stumme had suffered from high blood pressure. His body was found in the desert later; he had died of a heart attack while under heavy fire at the front.)

Immediately following Berndt's call, the Führer called from OKW headquarters. Was Rommel up to returning to North Africa? He was. Rommel left at once for Egypt.

Montgomery had launched his offensive on the night of October 23–24, 1942. It was intended to "eliminate

Rommel"[63] once and for all. History records the start of the British offensive as the Second Battle of El Alamein. The battle marked the beginning of the end of the Axis forces in North Africa.

"Monty," as Montgomery was popularly known, had planned his offensive for two months with meticulous care for the smallest details. He had trained his units in night movement and mine clearing, and he had worked out an elaborate and extensive plan for artillery support. Further, to confuse the enemy as to the time and place of his attack, Monty had devised complicated disinformation and deceptive measures. Most important, he had planned to take full advantage of his huge superiority in men, tanks, and guns.

Montgomery's Eighth Army now consisted of the Tenth, Thirteenth, and Thirtieth Corps with a total of 195,000 men and 1,029 tanks on line, 200 in reserve, and another 1,000 in repair shops. (Some 300 of Monty's tanks were Shermans, which Roosevelt had sent off to Africa after the fall of Tobruk.) Another 2,311 artillery pieces supported the Eighth Army, and the Royal Air Force controlled the skies.

By comparison, Rommel's *Panzerarmee Afrika* consisted of the *Deutsches Afrika Korps* (Fifteenth and Twenty-First Panzer Divisions), the Ninetieth and 164th Light Divisions, the Ramcke Parachute Brigade, the Italian Tenth, Twentieth, and Twenty-First Corps, and other Axis formations numbering 104,000 men (50,000 German and 54,000 Italian). Rommel could field 520 tanks and call on 1,219 artillery pieces for support.

Unlike all other battlefronts in the desert, both ends of the Alamein front were immune to flanking movements by either army. (Flanking movements around the enemy's southern flank had become a standard practice of both Axis and Allied armies in the desert.) Located between the sea at

General Sherman Tank

The American M4 series medium tank was arguably the most successful Allied tank of World War II—and certainly the most widely produced. The British nicknamed it the "General Sherman," which those who fought with it shortened to simply the "Sherman." Three hundred Shermans helped to defeat Field Marshal Erwin Rommel in the Second Battle of El Alamein in 1942. Later in the war, German tanks generally outgunned it—particularly the Panther and Tiger tanks. But because of the Sherman's superior maneuverability and greater availability, it could usually outfight its German adversaries.

Like its predecessor, the M3 "General Grant," the Sherman was hastily developed after events in Europe had demonstrated the obsolescence of light-gunned tanks early in the war. The U.S. Army's Ordnance Department completed the first Sherman prototype (T6) in September 1941, and the first combat models began rolling off production lines in July 1942. Total war production for the Sherman exceeded 49,000. It saw action in the Mediterranean, European, and South Pacific Theaters in World War II, and subsequently in the early Middle Eastern conflicts.

The Sherman was produced in a number of different models, and its specifications varied somewhat with each model. Specifications for the M4A1 version were as follows:

Length: 19.2 feet

Width: 8.5 feet

Height: 9 feet

Weight: 33.3 tons

Crew: 5

Main armament: 75-mm gun

Secondary armament: One .50-caliber and two .30-caliber machine guns

Engine: Continental 400 hp

Range: 100 miles

Speed: 24 mph

Armor: 1 in. (hull); 2 in. (turret)

The American M-4 series Sherman tank was arguably the most successful
Allied tank of World War II. Three hundred of these helped to defeat
Rommel in the Second Battle of El Alamein in 1942.

El Alamein in the north and the Qattara Depression—an impassable low area—in the south, the 37-mile front lent itself to a ready defense by either army.

Aware of Rommel's fuel shortage through Ultra intercepts and other intelligence means, Montgomery planned to fight what he called a "crumbling" battle: He meant to switch the emphasis of his attack from place to place, thus forcing Rommel to expend valuable fuel in reacting to British thrusts along the line. Rommel, because of his crippling fuel shortage, could neither advance nor retreat and was compelled to await Montgomery's long-expected attack.

To defend his position, Rommel had laid mines and booby traps in a five-mile-deep field called "Devil's Garden," and he had interlaced weaker Italian elements with German units along his defense line. He planned to hold back the Fifteenth Panzer and Littorio Divisions in the north, and the Twenty-First Panzer and Ariete in the south, with the Ninetieth Light Division in reserve. Rommel had only enough fuel to move his Fifteenth Panzers south or his Twenty-First Panzers north a single time—but not back—depending on the location of Montgomery's main assault. He had no margin for error.

Montgomery preceded his attack with a murderous artillery barrage at 9:40 P.M. on October 23. A thousand guns broke the silence of the desert night with an ear-splitting thunder unequaled since World War I, shaking the earth and pouring a firestorm of high explosives into the Devil's Garden and the Axis entrenchments beyond. Artillery shells touched off acres of mines and sent them rocketing skyward. Barbed-wire entanglements crumpled and disappeared. Blockhouses collapsed and bunkers caved in. Geysers of rock and sand spewed high into the air and fell on huddled troops below. Men died.

October 23, 1942 saw the start of a decisive British campaign against Rommel's forces. Massive Allied artillery barrages exploded many of Rommel's mines along the region known as the "Devil's Garden" and cleared the way for advancing British forces.

When the barrage lifted 20 minutes later, Montgomery launched the first phase of his offensive under a full moon. Appropriately, he called it "Operation Lightfoot."

To push through the minefield and neutralize the enemy's forward defenses, he led off with his infantry, followed by sappers—demolition experts. The sappers used long-handled mine detectors to clear lanes up to 24 feet wide—wide enough for tanks to pass through the minefield two abreast. They marked the cleared lanes with 120 miles of marker tape and lit them with 88,000 lamps for Monty's armor to pass through. (The artillery barrage destroyed thousands of mines, but Rommel had planted more than a half-million in his Devil's Garden, so plenty remained for the sappers to find and remove the hard way, many times the old-fashioned way—by prodding the sands with a bayonet.)

Montgomery's first goal was to establish a salient—a forward bulge in the Axis defense line—ten miles wide and five miles deep by dawn of October 24. To this end, his Thirtieth Corps struck Rommel's (Thoma's) left flank, while his Thirteenth Corps initiated a diversionary attack near the Qattara Depression to the south. Four hours later, his Tenth (armored) Corps advanced through two corridors that had been cleared by infantrymen of Thirtieth Corps. Despite their initial surprise, the Italian infantry fought back stubbornly, and a quick response by the Fifteenth Panzers almost stopped the British advance. Similarly, the Thirteenth Corps in the south made only slight gains.

Rommel arrived at his *Panzerarmee* headquarters at dusk on October 25. He found the situation untenable. It was, in fact, unwinnable. "Rommel could do nothing," Colonel Fritz Bayerlein, Rommel's chief of staff, said later. "He took over a battle in which all his reserves were already committed. No major decisions which could alter the course of events were possible." [64]

Although defeat appeared imminent, Rommel intended to make it a costly victory for the British. That night, he signaled all his troops: "I have taken command of the army again.—*Rommel*." [65] All that a commander could do, he would do.

The next day, Montgomery ceased his attack in the south and directed the weight of his army against the coastal area, where the Ninth Australian Division (Thirtieth Corps) threatened to force the German 164th Division into the sea. A brutal tank battle erupted and raged for a week in the minefields south of the coastal road and railroad, as both sides moved their armor up from the south. Rommel necessarily committed his tanks piecemeal. Short of fuel and under constant attack by the Royal Air Force, their numbers diminished rapidly. Rommel had no replacements, and he expected Montgomery to begin a major attack at any moment.

On October 29, Rommel, according to his diary, "decided that morning that if British pressure became too strong I would withdraw to the Fuka position before the battle had reached its climax." [66] The Fuka position was a fallback line that began at Fuka on the Mediterranean and ended, just as the Alamein line, at the Qattara Depression.

The next night, the Australians lashed out again toward the coast, striving to encircle the 164th Light Division. Rommel personally directed a counterattack by the Ninetieth Light Division and elements of the Twenty-First Panzers in an effort to stabilize the situation. The "Aussies" suffered frightful casualties but managed to hold firm against daunting odds, unrelenting Axis artillery, and bitter fighting. Rommel was making Monty pay for the gain of every square foot of sand. Montgomery began rethinking his strategy.

On November 1, the Royal Air Force struck back. "That day waves of British aircraft, each of 18 to 20 bombers, attacked our front north of Hill 28 [called Kidney Ridge by the British] no less than 34 times," Rommel recalled later. "The air was filled with hundreds of British fighters, and large numbers of R.A.F. fighter-bombers spent the day shooting-up our supply vehicles on the coast road." [67]

One hour into the next day, November 2, British big guns heralded the start of Montgomery's decisive drive, code-named "Operation Supercharge." High explosive shells from more than 800 cannon shattered the earth along a frontage only 4,000 yards south of Kidney Ridge. Monty's New Zealanders, behind a rolling artillery barrage, cleared a corridor through the minefield and the British First Armored Division churned through the Axis lines. (A rolling artillery barrage moves forward

In early November 1942, Montgomery's forces again pummeled Rommel's tanks with artillery fire. Short on reserves and with only a few dozen Panzers operational, the Desert Fox decided to withdraw. Although Hitler had ordered Rommel to stand fast on November 2, the German forces only lasted another day and a half before retreating.

at a safe distance ahead of advancing friendly troops.)

Rommel counterattacked with all his remaining panzer and infantry reserves and succeeded in checking the British advance—but not for long. By the end of the day, only 35 German "runners" (functional tanks) remained at Rommel's disposal. "This then," Rommel wrote later, "was the moment to get back to the Fuka line." [68] That night, he ordered his forces to withdraw along the coast to Fuka, 60 miles west of Alamein.

In the midst of his general retirement, however, he

received stunning news from Hitler. Via a radioed message, the Führer directed Rommel to stand fast. He said, in part:

> Superior [the British] may be, but the enemy are surely also at the end of their strength. It would not be the first time in history that will-power has triumphed over the stronger battalions of an enemy. To your troops therefore you can offer only one path—the path that leads to Victory or Death. *Sgd: Adolf Hitler.*[69]

Despite his horrendous losses, Rommel, good soldier that he was, could not bring himself to disobey the Führer's order. He immediately reversed his own order to withdraw and directed all units to stand and hold. His underfed and overmatched soldiers stood fast for another day and a half, but they had reached their limits.

In a diary entry written in his foxhole on the morning of November 3, a lieutenant in the 104th Panzer Grenadiers (armored infantry) captured the futility of their situation:

> We are here, a few grenadiers in our foxholes. The cold has passed, but hunger remains. Every 20 yards, lie a few men. Two anti-tank guns, that is all. And facing us, an armada of tanks.[70]

The next day, with the Eighth Army advancing all along the front, Rommel again ordered a withdrawal to the Fuka line. "So now it had come," Rommel wrote later, "the thing we had done everything in our power to avoid—our front broken and the fully motorized enemy streaming into our rear. Superior orders could no longer count. We had to save what there was to save."[71] What remained to be saved amounted to less than half of his army.

Rommel suffered enormous losses in the Second Battle of

Alamein: about 59,000 killed, wounded, and captured (including 34,000 Germans); 500 tanks; 400 guns; and innumerable other vehicles. Montgomery lost about 13,000 killed, wounded, and missing, and 432 of his tanks were knocked out of action (many of which were salvaged and repaired).

Strategically and psychologically, Montgomery's victory at Alamein represents one of World War II's most decisive victories. It saved the Suez Canal, marked the start of the Axis decline, and provided the overture for the Anglo-American invasion of North Africa four days later. Allied morale soared, and the British Empire rejoiced—it at long last had a victorious army and general. Finally, as Winston Churchill observed, "It might almost be said that before Alamein we never had a victory, while after Alamein we never had a defeat." [72]

As for Rommel's perspective on the battle, looking back on Alamein, he wrote, "I am conscious of only one mistake—that I did not circumvent the 'Victory or Death' order twenty-four hours earlier. Then the army would in all probability have been saved . . ." [73]

6

Last Act in Africa

After Alamein, many British commanders felt bitter over the high cost of victory. They believed that Montgomery's ardor to crush Rommel's forces through sheer force of numbers—that is, via the military dictum of proper application of overwhelming force—had resulted in the needless loss of too many lives. But Montgomery felt elated. "It was a fine battle," he told war correspondents. "Complete and absolute victory."[74] For Rommel, it was a total and irreversible defeat.

On November 4, 1942, Rommel and his *Panzerarmee Afrika*, living on borrowed time, began a long and punishing westward withdrawal. Rommel's masterful retirement, conserving most of what remained of his army, added to his reputation as a premier field general. Despite repeated orders from Hitler and Mussolini to stand fast, and in spite of critical fuel and ammunition shortages, Rommel managed to delay Montgomery's pursuit long enough to make good his escape.

Montgomery's critics argue that his initially lethargic pursuit—possibly induced by a post-battle "letdown"—allowed Rommel to slip through a series of "trap doors" in the ranks of Eighth Army elements that Montgomery had sent northwest to intercept Rommel, either west of Daba or farther west at Fuka. Montgomery held a different view. In his post-battle account, he asserted that "only the rain on 6th and 7th November saved them from complete annihilation."[75] Montgomery's critics dispute his assertion, pointing out that Rommel had already escaped by the time the rains came. In any event, after the rains, Montgomery's pursuit was further hampered not only by the impeding mud but also by insufficient fuel to maintain the chase.

By the end of November, Rommel had reached the Mersa el Brega defensive line in Libya. His army now stood some 600 miles west of El Alamein and 500 miles east of Tunis, the capital of Tunisia. Responding to an order from Mussolini—and agreed to by Hitler—to make a stand, he paused. "We had still received no strategic decision from the supreme German and Italian authorities on the future of the African theatre of war," [76] he noted later. That was about to change. Hitler summoned him home for a strategy session.

Meanwhile, three weeks earlier, an Anglo-American amphibious force had begun "Operation Torch"—the invasion of French Algeria and Morocco—on November 8. The Allies, under the overall command of U.S. Lieutenant General Dwight D. "Ike" Eisenhower, had landed in three sectors of the North African coast. In four days, the invaders overcame Vichy French defenders at Casablanca, in Morocco, and at Oran and Algiers in Algeria, and headed eastward.

Rommel's expertise delayed the British long enough for the Field Marshal and most of his remaining forces to escape. In the meantime, however, combined U.S. and British forces staged an amphibious landing in French Algeria and Morocco, quickly overwhelming any forces loyal to the Axis.

French forces in North Africa had sworn allegiance to the collaborative French government in Vichy, France. Under the terms of the Franco-German armistice in June 1940, the French garrisons in Morocco and Algeria were obligated to defend the French colonies against any Allied invasion attempts. This they did—but not for long.

The strategic aim of Operation Torch was to clear the Axis forces out of North Africa through linking the eastward-moving Torch forces with Montgomery's westward-advancing Eighth Army. This would effectively trap Rommel between two jaws of a vise. The Torch forces, fired by their initial successes and bursting with confidence, expected to cover the 450 miles from Algiers to Bizerte and Tunis in two weeks. But rain turned the already poor roads into quagmires. The eastward dash of the Allies slowed to a slog, and they failed to take advantage of Rommel's reverses in Egypt.

In the meantime, Field Marshal Albert Kesselring, German commander in chief in Italy, had reacted quickly to the new Allied threat. From nearby Sicily, he began pouring troops and supplies into Tunisia by sea and air. The Germans captured airfields in Tunis and Bizerte and seized control of the air. When the slow-moving Torch forces reached Tunisia, an outnumbered German contingent met them and halted their advance. Kesselring continued the Axis buildup and by year's end, German and Italian forces in Tunisia numbered 100,000.

Back in Germany, meanwhile, Rommel tried again to convince the Führer of the folly of continuing the fighting in North Africa. It would be better, he told Hitler, to pull the *Panzerarmee* out of Africa to fight again in Italy. "Africa cannot be held," [77] he said.

Hitler called him a defeatist and his troops cowards and launched into one of his familiar tirades. "You are suggesting precisely the same as my generals [on the Eastern Front] did last winter," he shouted. "They wanted to fall back on the German frontier. I refused to allow it, and events proved me right."[78] Hitler continued his rantings at length.

Rommel had earlier experienced grave misgivings about Germany's ability to win the war. Now, for the first time, he began to question both the Führer's rationality and his competence to lead Germany. He at last recognized that Hitler held the German people in contempt and cared nothing for the men who fought for him.

German generals who had made "defeatist" suggestions in Russia had been stood against a wall and shot. Although Rommel was risking a similar fate, he kept arguing in an effort to save his army from extinction. The situation in North Africa was hopeless, he said. Perhaps, Rommel suggested, the Führer would like to fly down to Africa and see for himself. Hitler fumed. "Go!" he screamed. "I have other things to do than talk to you."[79]

Rommel saluted and left, shutting the door behind him. Barely a moment later, the Führer came running after him and apologized. "You must excuse me," Hitler said, "I'm in a very nervous state. But everything is going to be all right."[80] He invited Rommel to return the next day to discuss the situation calmly. "It is impossible to think of the Afrika Korps being destroyed,"[81] the Führer assured him.

When Rommel returned the next day, Hitler turned the matter over to his second in command, *Reichsmarschall* (Reich Marshal) Hermann Göring. "Do anything you like," he told the corpulent Göring, "but see that the Afrika Korps is supplied with all that Rommel needs."[82] Göring told Hitler that he would attend to it himself— but he did not.

The rotund one escorted Rommel to Rome on his personal train and talked about nothing but the art treasures that he expected to acquire for his large collection. In Rome, Göring spent his time looking for paintings and sculpture. "He was planning how to fill his train with them," Rommel recalled with contempt. "He never tried to see any one on business or to do anything for me."[83]

All was not lost, however. Rommel proposed a plan to withdraw his *Panzerarmee* through Buerat and Tripoli and into Tunisia. From there, he could join forces with the new German arrivals in Tunis and Bizerte and spring a new offensive against the green American invaders. Moreover, Rommel pointed out, the Tunisian ports were much closer to his sources of supply in Italy. Göring liked the proposal, but Field Marshal Kesselring did not. In the end, Mussolini approved Rommel's withdrawal but only to the Buerat line, 200 miles east of Tripoli.

Hermann Göring, *Reichsmarschall* of Germany and Hitler's second in command, was ordered by the Führer to give Rommel any material assistance he needed. Göring, however, ignored the order, spending his time enlarging his collection of pillaged art treasures.

On December 2, Rommel returned to Libya to play out his last act in Africa. He was by then convinced that Göring was mad and that Hitler was not far behind. Four days later—with the Eighth Army already massing for a new attack—the Italian infantry began pulling out of the

Mersa el Brega line after dark. The rest of the *Panzerarmee* followed them to the Buerat line over the next nine days. Montgomery commenced his new attack with the usual artillery barrage on the night of December 11. In the morning, he found the Mersa el Brega line empty.

Two weeks later in the west, General Eisenhower conceded all hope of seizing control of Tunisia that winter. In a "bitter decision," [84] he concluded that any further offensive operations would have to wait until after the two-month rainy season. Rommel, unaware of Ike's decision, agonized over the possibility that the Americans would capture Tunisia and cancel any chance that he might still have of linking up with the new German forces there.

In the east, advance elements of Montgomery's army reached the Buerat line on December 29. On the final day of 1942, Mussolini authorized Rommel to make a *slow* fighting withdrawal out of Libya and into Tunisia.

During the first few days of 1943, supplies for Rommel arrived in Tunis—but no gasoline. He had no choice except to evacuate the Buerat line on January 15 and retreat to a new line that extended from Tarhuna to Homs on the coast. It was the last defense line before Tripoli itself. Little work had been done on it, however, prompting Rommel to remark to an Italian staff officer, "We can't really expect to hold off the enemy in the Homs line for more than two days." [85] He held out for four days and fell back to Tripoli.

On January 22, in the face of Montgomery's unrelenting drive, Rommel pulled out again and retired into Tunisia. Four days later, he established *Panzerarmee* headquarters west of Ben Gardane. That same day, January 26, Rommel received word from the Italian High Command that he was to be relieved of duty because of his health. An Italian, General Giovanni Messe, was en route from the Russian Front to replace him. Rommel was to select the time of his own relief, but not until after he had reached the Mareth line.

The long retreat of some 1,500 miles had taken its toll on Rommel. He had been suffering with headaches, stomach distress, nervous exhaustion, and depression. But his health was not the real reason for his relief. Rather, it was because he had—in defiance of orders—repeatedly left defensive positions prematurely to spare his army from senseless destruction. Relief of command was the price of his disobedience. But Rommel had yet to play out his role in the North African theater.

On February 8, Rommel noted in his journal: "I've decided only to give up command of the army on orders, regardless of the state of my health. With the situation as it is, I intend to stick it out to the limit."[86] Despite the criticism of his superiors, Rommel had, in holding his army intact during his 1,500-mile retirement, accomplished nothing short of a miracle. Tunisia offered new opportunities, and he now looked forward to returning to the offensive.

In Tunisia, the weight of the Allied forces was concentrated in the north, oriented toward Bizerte and Tunis. They faced the Fifth Panzer Army—the new German force of some 100,000 troops—under Colonel General Jürgen von Arnim. Between them rose the Eastern Dorsale mountain range, running generally from north to south about 60 miles inland. With Rommel's *Panzerarmee Afrika* now positioned along the Mareth line to the south, only 200 miles separated the two Axis armies. To the west of Rommel, at the south end of the Eastern Dorsale, the inexperienced American Second Corps faced him.

Concerned that the Allies might push through to Tunis and cut off his source of supplies and convinced that Montgomery would not reach the Mareth line before March, Rommel decided to attack the Americans and instill in them "an inferiority complex of no mean order."[87] Afterward, he planned to double back and meet Montgomery's anticipated challenge at the Mareth line.

**With Rommel in failing health, German forces in North Africa
were divided in two—those commanded by Rommel in the west,
and those by General Jürgen von Arnim (seen here) in the east.
Their planned two-pronged assault lacked central coordination
and allowed Allied forces to regroup.**

On February 9, Kesselring flew in from Italy and
worked out a vague attack plan with Rommel and Arnim.
The plan called for a two-pronged assault with Arnim's
well-equipped army advancing through the Said Pass in the
Eastern Dorsale toward the towns of Sidi Bou Zid and
Sbeitla, 15 miles west and 35 miles northwest of the pass,

respectively. Meanwhile, Rommel was to target Gafsa farther south. But the plan had a serious flaw: Kesselring flew back to Italy, and the agreed-upon operation was left without an overall commander in the field. As a result, Arnim and Rommel acted independently.

Arnim moved first, attacking the Faid Pass on February 14. He met troops of Major General Lloyd R. Fredendall's U.S. Second Corps and found them ill prepared and poorly positioned to repulse his onslaught. He destroyed two American battalions, each containing armor, artillery, and infantry. The rest of Second Corps retreated hastily across the waist of Tunisia to the Western Dorsales, a parallel mountain chain, and turned to face their pursuers. But Arnim delayed pressing his attack until the night of February 16.

"On the morning of the 17th February, the division [the re-equipped Twenty-First Panzer Division that now formed a part of Arnim's Fifth Panzer Army] was in position in front of Sbeitla," Rommel noted later. "But the delay had enabled the Americans to organise some sort of a defence and they now fought back skillfully and bitterly. If Ziegler, who was commanding the 21st Panzer Division's operation, had only followed up his success at Sidi Bouzid immediately on his own initiative, he would not have had to fight so hard for Sbeitla."[88] Despite stiffening American resistance, Sbeitla fell to the Germans that night. In their four-day advance, the Panzers had captured 1,600 Americans and 150 tanks.

Meanwhile, after Arnim had started his advance on the Said Pass, American and French forces withdrew from Gafsa, and elements of Rommel's *Afrika Korps* and the Italian Centauro Armored Division occupied the town without a fight on February 15. At Rommel's direction, they advanced and captured Feriana and the airfields at Thelepte two days later.

Rommel now eyed the town of Tebessa—a major Allied communications and supply base just across the frontier in Algeria. He pressed the *Commando Supremo* (Supreme Command) in Italy for authority to continue on to Tebessa. Rommel wanted to seize Tebessa and strike deep into his enemy's rear. But the Supreme Command directed him not to Tebessa but to Thala and then to Le Kef. Rommel was shocked. "A thrust along that line was far too close to the front and was bound to bring us up against the strong enemy reserves," [89] he wrote later.

Orders were orders, however, and Rommel began advancing into the Western Dorsales via the Kasserine Pass on February 19. Kasserine Pass, a narrow corridor through the mountains, provided a gateway to both Tebessa and Thala. At the same time, Ziegler's Twenty-First Panzers received orders to move ahead toward Sbiba, where three days of furious fighting between British-French-American forces and the Germans resulted in a standoff. In the meantime, after being temporarily halted in Kasserine Pass, Rommel broke through the U.S. First Armored Division defenses on February 20.

British General Sir Harold Alexander, Eisenhower's deputy supreme commander, reacted quickly to the Axis attacks and moved reinforcements into blocking positions on the Thala and Sbiba roads. The reinforcements halted further thrusts by Arnim's Tenth and Twenty-First Panzer Divisions, and the U.S. First Armored Division rallied to check further progress by Rommel's *Afrika Korps* east of Tebessa.

Rommel, with his supplies down to one day of ammunition and six days of food—and almost out of gasoline for his vehicles—called off his attack on February 22. He withdrew his forces during the night before the Allies realized that they had left. Field Marshal Kesselring later expressed surprise and disappointment at Rommel's decision to pull out of Kasserine. "Nothing of his usual passionate will to command could be felt." [90]

While it was true that Rommel was then suffering from depression and severe desert sores, it was also true—according to Rommel's papers—that Kesselring had met with Rommel and other German field commanders in a strategy session on February 21. "We agreed," wrote Rommel, "that a continuation of the attack towards Le Kef held no prospect of success and decided to break off the offensive in stages." [91]

Rommel had failed to score a strategic victory, but—despite his poor mental and physical health—he had achieved a stunning tactical success. He had driven American and French forces 50 miles across the Sbeitla plain into the Western Dorsales. On the Americans alone, he had inflicted losses of more than 6,000 troops, 183 tanks, and 200 guns. And he had lost fewer than 1,000 men and 20 tanks.

The Battle of Kasserine Pass was a damaging embarrassment to the Allies—but not a mortal blow. With a single command—or with more help from Arnim—Rommel might have accomplished much more. Many strategists believe that the Allies escaped from a major disaster because Arnim and Rommel acted independently. Yet, it was a victory for Rommel—his last.

On February 23, Rommel turned over command of his German-Italian Panzer Army (the renamed *Panzerarmee Afrika*) to General Messe and moved up to command the newly created *Armeegruppe Afrika* (Army Group Africa). He now held authority over both Messe and Arnim. Strangely enough, Kesselring had recommended him for the new position. As subsequent events would show, however, it was a command in name only.

On February 26, Arnim launched an independent offensive in northern Tunisia toward Beja and Medjez el

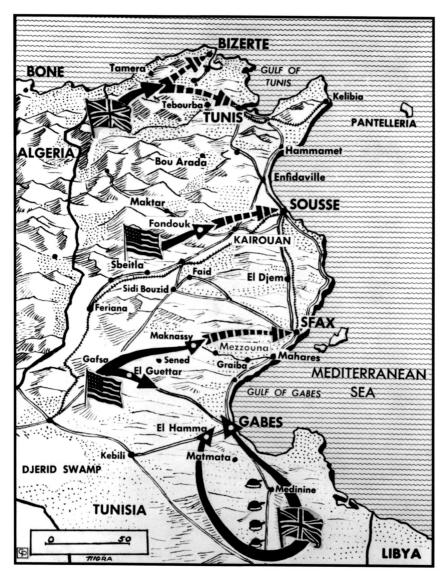

This map shows the path of Allied advances and battles against Rommel's forces in Tunisia in an attempt to cut off the Desert Fox's escape routes.

Bab that bogged down in a marshy valley and resulted in heavy German losses. Rommel, who later criticized Arnim's move, had not learned of the offensive until two days before it started and therefore had not contributed to its planning or authorization.

On March 6, Messe, who like Arnim was dealing directly with Kesselring in Italy, attacked Montgomery's Eighth Army at Medenine, where it was assembling for an attack of its own against the Mareth line. Montgomery administered a crushing defeat to Messe, and it became clear to Rommel that the Axis forces could delay the inevitable no longer.

Three days later, Rommel flew to Rome and met with Mussolini and Kesselring. He told them that further resistance in North Africa was not only useless but rather "was now plain suicide."[92] They referred him to Hitler.

Rommel repeated his views to Hitler and reiterated the importance of conserving their assets in North Africa for the defense of Europe. He in fact pleaded with the Führer to save his troops in Africa. Hitler responded by awarding Rommel with Oak Leaves with Swords and Diamonds to his Knight's Cross and ordering him on extended sick leave.

After two years of glorious victories and humiliating defeats, the curtain had rung down on the Desert Fox's last act in Africa.

7

The Desert Fox in Normandy

After his latest audience with Hitler, Rommel returned to Semmering to begin his rehabilitation. He felt further disillusioned with the Führer and terribly distressed over the war's eventual outcome. From the mountain resort in Austria, he watched with dismay as the North African campaign rushed to its conclusion.

On May 6, 1943, the Americans advanced on Medjez el Bab under a massive air attack and rolling artillery barrage. They drove deep into the German lines and all but annihilated the Fifteenth Panzer Division. "The front collapsed," wrote Rommel. "[T]here were no more arms and no ammunition and it was all over. The Army surrendered."[93]

Tunis and Bizerte fell simultaneously the next day. Just as

Rommel's repeated efforts to convince Hitler of the futility of continued military action in North Africa went unheeded. Instead, Allied forces broke through German lines, resulting in one of the largest German defeats of the war. Here, British soldiers bring a six-pounder gun up a mountain in Tunisia.

Rommel had predicted, the Allied conquerors captured some 250,000 prisoners, including General Arnim, who had assumed command of *Armeegruppe Afrika*. The six-month Tunisian campaign cost the Axis forces about 40,000 dead and wounded. American casualties numbered 18,500, including 2,184 killed. British casualties totaled 33,000.

The German losses almost rose to the level of Hitler's losses at Stalingrad, on the Eastern Front, a few months earlier. Hitler, lamenting his North African losses later, told Rommel, "I should have listened to you before." [94]

Two months later, using Tunisia as a springboard, the Allies invaded Sicily on July 10, 1943. They planned to use the big Italian island as a stepping-stone to Italy itself. Rommel foresaw only gloomy prospects for the future of Italy—and for the German war effort. "The moment the first Allied soldier set foot on Italian soil," he noted, "Mussolini was finished and the rebirth of the Roman Empire was probably over for good." [95]

Even more troubling to Rommel was the realization that Germany's "star was in decline and the knowledge of how little our command measured up to the trials which lay ahead." [96] He now suspected that Hitler no longer believed that Germany could win the war. Worse, the Führer seemed bent on self-destruction and intent upon dragging the nation down with him in the ruins of the Third Reich—the third (German) empire that he had boasted would last for 1,000 years—but the destruction of an empire takes time. Meanwhile, Hitler, anticipating Italy's potential surrender, posted Rommel to the north of Italy as commander of Army Group B.

Hitler believed that he could not defend the entire length of Italy in the event of an Italian surrender. Rommel's mission was to establish a defensive line in the northern Apennines to protect the agriculturally and industrially rich Po Valley. If Italy pulled out of the war, his armies were to occupy all the vital passes and railways in the north, while Field Marshal Kesselring withdrew his forces in the south to Rommel's defensive line. At that point, Rommel was to become commander in chief of German forces in Italy.

On July 25, only 15 days after the Allied invasion of Sicily, Mussolini was forced to resign. His successor, Marshal Pietro Badoglio, surrendered in secret negotiations with the Allies on September 3. The Allies announced Italy's capitulation on September 8 and invaded the Italian mainland the next day. British forces landed at the toe and heel of the Italian "boot," while British and American units splashed ashore at Salerno, some 26 miles east-southeast of Naples on the west coast of the Italian peninsula—or about a quarter of the way up the boot.

After quickly securing Kesselring's rear, Rommel

established his headquarters at Lake Garda, in east Lombardy, on September 12. Kesselring engaged the Allies at Salerno long enough to recover his troops to the south, then began a gradual, masterful withdrawal up the peninsula. Then the two field marshals disagreed on what to do next.

At a strategy meeting at Hitler's headquarters, Kesselring proposed defending Italy south of Rome, pointing out that the terrain afforded excellent maneuver conditions. Rommel, fearing that Allied seaborne operations along the length of the peninsula might outflank Kesselring and jeopardize the vital Po Valley, recommended his immediate retirement from the southern provinces to the Apennine line, 90 miles north of Rome.

Hitler, irrespective of his original thinking, sided with Kesselring. In his twisted view of the war, he still counted on the eventual collapse of the Allied war effort. "There will come a certain point of time when we can no longer win the war by conquering the world," he said, "but only by keeping the war dragging on until the other side gives in." [97]

Despite Kesselring's stellar defensive effort in the south, Rommel held stubbornly to his views until he again earned Hitler's disfavor as a defeatist. On November 6, Hitler named Kesselring—instead of Rommel—as supreme commander in Italy. At the same time, he informed Rommel of his reassignment to France on a special mission to inspect the coastal defenses in the west and make recommendations.

Hitler underscored the task's importance to the Reich. "When the enemy invades in the west it will be the moment of decision in this war," he said. "And the moment must turn to our advantage. We must ruthlessly extract every ounce of effort from Germany." [98] Hitler implied that when the invasion began, command of the western defense forces would shift from 68-year-old Field Marshal Karl R. Gerd von Rundstedt to Rommel, who was now 52. The Führer, however, neglected to inform Rundstedt.

At last out of North Africa, Rommel traveled to the shores of Western Europe to inspect Hitler's "Atlantic Wall," a string of battlements designed to prevent an Allied invasion by sea. Rommel used his expertise and reputation to strengthen the wall and boost the spirits of German forces along the coast.

On November 21, Rommel left Italy and took leave in Herrlingen. In December, he boarded a special train and began his inspection tour in Denmark. A skeleton staff from Italy—designated Army Group B z.v.B ("for Special Purposes")—accompanied him on his tour of the "Atlantic Wall," Hitler's name for the string of German defensive emplacements along the shoreline of Western Europe.

The Atlantic Wall had been under construction by the Todt Organization—a civilian engineering firm—since 1942, using Germans and thousands of forced laborers. Hitler described the Wall as "a belt of strongpoints and gigantic fortifications" and boasted that it was "impregnable against every enemy."[99] After his initial inspection tour, Rommel scoffed at its alleged invulnerability and set to work improving it.

On December 18, the Desert Fox returned to Normandy, the scene of his earlier triumphs with the Spook Division during the German blitzkrieg of 1940. The next day, he wrote to Lucie, "I'm going to throw myself into this new job with everything I've got, and I'm going to see it turns out a success."[100] With renewed vigor and dedication, he set about turning the Atlantic Wall into a re-created Alamein line—only 50 times longer.

Everywhere he went, he brought new hope and spirit to the coastal defenders and improved the defenses. According to the official U.S. Army history of the Normandy campaign, "Rommel's reputation in combat was a stimulant and a dramatization of the new importance assigned to the west."[101] Rommel planned to create an impenetrable band of mines and bunkers, six miles wide, along the entire Atlantic Wall.

Bushy-browed Lieutenant General Doctor Wilhelm Meise, Rommel's engineering expert, listened in rapt attention as Rommel rattled off his plans:

> I want anti-personnel mines, anti-tank mines, anti-paratroop mines—I want mines to sink ships and mines to sink landing craft. . . . I want some minefields designed so that our own infantry can cross them, but not the enemy. I want mines that detonate when a wire is tripped; mines that explode when a wire is cut; mines that can be remote controlled, and mines that will blow up when a beam of light is interrupted. Some of them must be encased in non-ferrous metals [metal containing no iron, such as aluminum], so that the enemy's mine detectors won't register them.[102]

Rommel personally supervised the construction of additional strong points. In six months, Rommel would triple the number of mines along the Atlantic Wall to about 6 million. And he would add all manner of ingenious obstacles and impedance devices to the anticipated landing areas: ramming cones to wreck invading landing craft, hundreds of thousands of tetrahedrons on the beaches (vehicle/tank obstacles built of steel girders), booby traps, sharp posts implanted in fields to prevent glider landings, and many more.

Beyond his greatness as a general, Meise said later, Rommel was the greatest engineer of World War II. "There was nothing I could teach him. He was my master." [103] But even Rommel could not work miracles, and shortages of concrete and other materials and insufficient time prevented him from completing the Atlantic Wall to his satisfaction.

Hobart's Funnies

Field Marshal Erwin Rommel's inventive mind gave birth to many defensive obstacles and devices that lined the beaches of Normandy. To counter many of Rommel's creative obstructions, the British called upon retired Major General Percy Hobart. A pioneer in tank warfare during the 1930s, Hobart was serving as a corporal in the British Home Guard when asked to develop tank innovations for use in the coming Normandy invasion.

The DD (Duplex Drive) Sherman tank formed the centerpiece for a subsequent array of ingenious tank modifications and accouterments developed by the reactivated general. Known as a "swimming tank," the DD was equipped with a canvas flotation device, or "skirt," that both hid the tank and kept it watertight. A specially designed and constructed exhaust system rendered the DD a truly amphibious vehicle. Some 900 DDs lumbered ashore at British-assigned beaches (Gold, Juno, and Sword) on D day.

Additional innovations conceived by Hobart's fertile mind included: "flail" tanks that used weighted chains on a rotating drum extended in front of the tank to "flail" a path through minefields; "dozer" tanks fitted with bulldozer blades to clear obstacles under fire; "arks," turretless tanks with front and rear ramps that would drive into an obstacle, lower both ramps, and form a bridge for other tanks to drive over; multipurpose tanks with a variety of devices for crossing ditches, breaching concrete obstacles, and clearing rubble; flamethrowing tanks; and many more.

These inventions were collectively known as "Hobart's Funnies," but they did not appear at all funny to the Germans.

On January 15, Hitler strengthened and reconstituted Army Group B headquarters and placed Rommel in command of the Seventh and Fifteenth Armies in France and the Low Countries (Netherlands, Belgium, and Luxembourg). He still functioned under the authority of Field Marshal Rundstedt, the designated OB West (the German abbreviation for *Oberbefehlshaber West*—the Commander in Chief, West, or his headquarters). But from then on, Rommel, with a direct line of communications with Hitler himself, became the dominant personality in the west.

As was often the case, Rommel and his immediate superior held different views on the most suitable strategy to fit the current situation. "From his extensive experience with landing operations in Africa and Italy, Rommel had formulated the opinion that an enemy, once landed and prospected by covering fire from naval artillery and from the air, was extremely difficult to throw back into the sea," explained Lieutenant General Max Pemsel, chief of staff of the German Seventh Army. "It was therefore a proposition of making the coastal defenses so strong in manpower and equipment that the enemy could never gain a foothold on the shore."[104]

Rundstedt, on the other hand, advocated holding a powerful mobile force in strategic reserve until the site of the main Allied landing force was identified. At that time a classic counterstroke in depth would be launched to overwhelm and destroy the enemy beachhead. Rommel faulted this strategy on grounds that the enemy's total mastery of the air would prevent any strategic reserves from moving to the battlefield once the invasion had begun.

Hitler never settled on either plan. His indecision was to result in a cross between both concepts that ultimately would produce disastrous consequences. Rundstedt, true to his plan, assembled a centralized armored reserve for rapid deployment to the invasion site once it became known. Rommel, in accord with his contrasting notion, placed the bulk of his armies—which consisted mostly of infantry without transportation—close to the most probable landing locations.

Both Rommel and Rundstedt expected the Allies to land somewhere in the Pas de Calais—the Strait of Dover—region of France. Through a massive program of deception and disinformation, the Allies misled the Germans into believing that the main Allied forces would indeed land in the Pas de Calais, but the Allies actually planned to land on five beaches—code-named Utah, Omaha, Gold, Juno, and Sword—in the Normandy area of France. American General Dwight D. Eisenhower was appointed supreme commander of the Allied invasion forces.

"Operation Overlord"—the code name for the Allied invasion plan—called for several objectives to be achieved within three months. The first objective of the Allied invaders was to drive inland from the beaches and secure a sizeable lodgment in western France between the Seine and Loire Rivers. Once established, this lodgment would serve as an operating base on the continent from which to break through the enemy's containing forces. After pausing briefly to build up their forces, the Allies would then press eastward to the German frontier, span the Rhine River, and advance into the Ruhr Valley, the heart of German industry.

Eisenhower ultimately set June 6, 1944, as D day—the start date for the Allied invasion of Western Europe.

On June 4, a stormy day that seemed to preclude any danger of an Allied invasion attempt, Rommel left his headquarters in France and motored to Herrlingen to spend his wife's fiftieth birthday with her. From there, he planned to drive on to Hitler's retreat above the Bavarian town of Berchtesgaden. He hoped to convince the Führer of his need for two more panzer divisions, an antiaircraft corps, and a mortar brigade in Normandy. Rommel had no way of knowing it, of course, but it was already too late.

Shortly after midnight on Tuesday, June 6, 1944, British

Shortly after Lucie Rommel's 50ᵗʰ birthday, the Atlantic Wall was tested when Allied forces launched a massive landing on June 6, 1944. Here, American paratroopers prepare for the Normandy invasion known as D day.

and American airborne troops began dropping into the fields of Normandy. The invasion was on!

At 10:15 that morning, the telephone rang in Rommel's Herrlingen residence. It was Lieutenant General Hans Speidel, his chief of staff, calling from France: The invasion had started. Rommel went pale. "I'll return at once!"[105] he snapped. Rommel left at once for Normandy with his aide, Captain Helmuth Lang.

On the way to France, Rommel told Lang, "I was right all along, all along."[106] He had earlier told his aide, "The first 24 hours of the invasion will be decisive . . . for the Allies as well as Germany it will be the longest day."[107] And he would miss most of it.

Rommel arrived at the battlefront that night and tried to seal off and destroy the Allied beachhead, while Rundstedt attempted to organize his armored reserves for a run at the beaches. Just as Rommel had anticipated, however, Allied air forces minimized German troop movements to the front and knocked out the headquarters of the panzers. Rommel's strategy, handicapped as it was, managed to confine the Allies to a thin swath of coastline.

By mid-June, Rommel had become convinced that the enemy foothold was too firmly implanted to uproot. He started to think of abandoning Normandy and falling back to a more defensible line at the approaches to Germany, but Hitler would have none of it.

Both Rundstedt and Rommel met with Hitler in Soissons on June 17 and again in Berchtesgaden on June 29. On both occasions the field marshals asked for more freedom of action on the battlefield regarding the use of reserves and the authority to shorten their lines of defense. And both times Hitler criticized their shortcomings and tactical handling of the situation. He ordered them to defend their positions to the last man. They did—and German losses continued to mount at an astounding rate.

On July 2, Rundstedt called Field Marshal Wilhelm Keitel, chief of the German High Command, to inform him of the growing futility of the situation in Normandy and of the war itself. Keitel, distraught, asked, "What shall we do?"[108]

"Make peace, you fools," Rundstedt replied. "What else can you do."[109] The next morning, Hitler replaced Rundstedt with Field Marshal Günther von Kluge.

When Rommel learned of Rundstedt's dismissal, he said, "I will be next."[110] But Hitler left him in command of Army Group B. The Führer did, however, warn Kluge of Rommel's growing pessimism and tendency to disobey orders.

As the new OB West, Kluge began his duties by announcing his commitment to an "unconditional holding of the present defense line."[111] Kluge's optimism faded fast and he soon came to share Rommel's dejection over the military situation.

Rommel had ample reason to feel downcast. By mid-July, the German field army had lost 100,000 men in Normandy, while receiving only 6,000 replacements. Given such an imbalance between losses and new forces, it became clear that Germany would soon run out of soldiers to man the battle line. Something had to be done to persuade the Führer to step aside so that more rational minds might negotiate a peace with the British and Americans before the hated Soviets invaded Germany.

On July 15, in a conversation with Rommel, Colonel Elmar Warning, the chief of operations for the Seventeenth Luftwaffe Division and a former member of Rommel's staff in the *Afrika Korps*, asked about the true situation. "Field Marshal, what's really going to happen here? Twelve German divisions are trying to contain the whole front."[112]

Rommel replied with absolute candor. "I'll tell you something," he said. "Field Marshal von Kluge and I have sent the Führer an ultimatum. Militarily, the war can't be won and he must make a political decision."[113]

Warning could scarcely believe his ears. "And what if the Führer refuses?"[114]

"Then," Rommel said, "I open the west front. There would only be one important matter left—that the Anglo-Americans reach Berlin before the Russians."[115] Two days later, fate intervened to spare Rommel from opening the gates to Germany to his enemies.

On July 17, while Rommel was returning to his headquarters after inspecting the First SS Panzer Corps, two British fighter-bombers attacked his open touring car on a secondary road from Livarot to Vimoutiers. The enemy planes roared in low and opened fire within 500 yards, wounding Rommel's driver. Glass fragments struck Rommel in the face and his head slammed against the windshield. Darkness engulfed him instantly.

The Desert Fox had fought his last battle in Normandy.

"Across the Havoc of War"

Rommel awakened at a military hospital in Bernay, about 25 miles away from the scene of the attack on his touring car by British fighter-bombers. "The doctors there," as his aide, Captain Hellmuth Lane, wrote later, "diagnosed severe injuries to the skull—a fracture at the base, two fractures on the temple and the cheek-bone destroyed, a wound in the left eye, wounds from glass and concussion."[116]

Doctors did not expect the field marshal to live. But Rommel had not the slightest intention of dying. In the light of later events, he might have wished at some point that he had. And he no doubt reflected on the irony of those events during his slow recovery over the next two months.

On July 17, 1944, with the war in Europe rapidly turning for the Allies, British fighter-bombers opened fire on Rommel's car, severely injuring him. Three days later, conspirators launched a failed attempt to kill Hitler with a bomb at the Führer's headquarters.

On July 20, 1944, three days after Rommel was injured, Hitler summoned his top military aides to a conference at his *Wolfsschanze* (Wolf's Lair) field headquarters at Rastenburg, East Prussia. Lieutenant Colonel Claus Philipp Schenk Graf (Count) von Stauffenberg, chief of staff of the German Replacement Army, was among the attendees. The count, a disabled, one-armed veteran of the North African campaign, was also a key conspirator in "Operation Valkyrie"—a plot to kill Hitler.

Most of the organizers of Valkyrie were high-ranking military officers. All were patriots. With the Soviets advancing all along the Eastern Front, and the British and the Americans threatening to break out of Normandy, they had come to accept the certainty of Germany's defeat. They hoped that Hitler's death would clear the way for a negotiated surrender and thus spare Germany its final agony.

Stauffenberg entered the conference room in Hitler's bunker at the Wolf's Lair, left a briefcase with a bomb under the heavy oak conference table, and discreetly slipped outside the building. When the meeting commenced, Lieutenant Colonel Heinz Brandt, assistant to the chief of army operations, inadvertently nudged the count's briefcase with his foot. Annoyed, he reached under the table and shifted the briefcase to the other side of a thick oaken table support. The colonel's simple act of annoyance saved the Führer's life, but not his own.

At 12:42 P.M., an explosion rocked Hitler's bunker. Brandt, two other officers, and a stenographer were killed, but Hitler was only slightly injured. The thick table support had shielded him from the blast. Stauffenberg, who had lingered outside, watched as a cloaked body was hauled out of the bunker on a stretcher. The count assumed that it was the Führer's corpse and flew at once to Berlin to join other conspirators who were to have seized the Supreme Command Headquarters there.

At about 1:00 P.M., the first news to reach Berlin indicated that Hitler was dead and calls began going out across a network of Valkyrie conspirators: *"Attentat! Führer ist tot!"*[117] But within minutes, Field Marshal Wilhelm Keitel, who had survived the blast at Rastenburg, ordered a corrective statement sent to Berlin: The Führer was alive! Then the line went dead. In the confusion, many of the conspirators revealed themselves but failed to seize control of the government. By the time they learned the truth, it was too late.

The plot had failed.

Numerous plots on the Führer's life had failed in the past, but this time he reacted murderously. "I will smash and destroy these criminals who have presumed to stand in the way of Providence and myself!" Hitler screamed in rage. "They deserve nothing but ignominious death! And I shall give it to them! This time the full measure will be paid by all who are involved, and by their families."[118] Rommel, however marginally, was one of those involved.

Rommel had learned of the plot against Hitler through contacts with several of the conspirators and veiled hints of an impending assassination attempt. Although he had on occasion guardedly approved of Hitler's removal from power, he had never condoned his murder. A better solution, he felt, would be to incarcerate him. "The Hitler legend will never be destroyed until the German people know the whole truth,"[119] he said. Rommel's injuries shielded him from Hitler's wrath, but only temporarily.

The Führer meted out swift—and often savage—penalties to most of the Valkyrie conspirators. Some 200 plotters were shot, hanged, or, in some cases, brutally strangled with piano wire and hung up on great meat hooks. The executioners filmed much of their handiwork for Hitler's repeated viewing and lasting enjoyment.

Stauffenberg's superior, Colonel General Friedrich Fromm, commander in chief of the German Replacement Army, executed Count von Stauffenberg and retired General Ludwig Beck, the prime organizer of the plot, before midnight on July 20. "Long live eternal Germany,"[120] Stauffenberg shouted before he fell. Fromm, a crafty schemer who had worked both sides of the conspiracy issue, was himself later tried for cowardice and shot on March 7, 1945.

The next day, General Karl Heinrich von Stülpnagel, the military governor of France, was summoned to Berlin to explain why he had ordered the arrest of German security personnel in Paris on the day of the assassination attempt. He stopped at Verdun on the way to Berlin and shot himself but succeeded only in blinding himself. Later in Berlin, while delirious, he kept repeating "Rommel!"[121] time and time again. Stülpnagel was eventually hanged with piano wire, but his ravings had already implicated Rommel in the plot.

Doctor Carl Gördeler, a former mayor of Leipzig and the civilian head of the Valkyrie conspiracy, also incriminated Rommel—and everyone else he knew—when captured and tortured by the Gestapo (a contraction of _Geheime Staatpolizei_, or Secret State Police). The Gestapo now had sufficient cause to close in on Rommel.

On July 24, Rommel was transferred to a military hospital at Le Vesinet, a suburb of Paris, because the German lines at nearby Caen had begun to collapse. In early August, he was discharged and sent home to continue his medical treatment and convalescence at Herrlingen. Upon seeing Rommel's injuries, Professor Albrecht, a noted brain specialist, said, "No man can be alive with wounds like that."[122] Rommel was not only alive, he was growing stronger each day. As he grew stronger, visiting friends kept him apprised of the latest developments in the Valkyrie investigations.

On August 15, Hitler replaced Field Marshal Günther von Kluge at OB West with Field Marshal Walther Model and summoned Kluge to Berlin. Kluge, of course, had been a signatory to Rommel's "ultimatum" to Hitler. While en route to Berlin, Kluge stopped at Verdun and took poison. Kluge died within a short walk of the spot where Stülpnagel had blinded himself.

Here, General Alexander von Falkenhausen—a conspirator in the assassination plot against Hitler—pleads his case in the People's Court in Berlin. Although sentenced to death, von Falkenhausen was freed by American troops shortly before his execution.

On September 6, Hans Speidel, Rommel's old friend and chief of staff, visited him at Herrlingen. It turned out to be the last time that they saw each other. The next day, the Gestapo arrested Speidel. Although he had been a conspirator, he managed, with the help of influential friends, to survive the Gestapo's inquisition and the war. Rommel now understood that he would not.

A few days after Speidel's arrest, Eugen Maier, chief of the Nazi Party in Ulm, visited Rommel and spoke of an ultimate German victory under Hitler's guidance. "Victory!" Rommel snapped. "Why don't you look at the map? The British are here, the Americans are here, the Russians are here. What is the use of talking about victory?"[123]

"If we couldn't have faith in our Führer then whom could we trust!"[124] Maier said.

Angered, Rommel replied, "You can't have any faith in him at all. Since I saw the Führer in 1942 I have come to realize that his mental faculties have steadily declined."[125]

"You should not say things like that, Field Marshal," Maier cautioned. "You will have the Gestapo after you — if they are not after you already."[126]

On October 7, Rommel received a summons requesting him to appear at an important conference in Berlin three days later. A special train would be sent to pick him up in Ulm. He had been expecting the summons and knew that it would be a journey from which he would not return. Rommel respectfully declined to attend the meeting on the basis of his poor health, but destiny's clock was ticking for the field marshal.

Six days later, a telephone call for Rommel came from the headquarters of War District Five in Stuttgart. Rommel was out. Rudolf Loistl, his soldier-servant, took the call: Lieutenant General Wilhelm Burgdorf, the army's chief personnel officer, was to arrive at the field marshal's home in Herrlingen the next day. He would be accompanied by Major General Ernst Maisel, chief legal officer of the personnel branch.

Burgdorf, a large, red-faced man, was known as "the gravedigger of the German Officer Corps."[127] And since July 20, Maisel, a somewhat shorter man with a long, pointed nose and foxlike ears, had been investigating officers suspected of conspiring to assassinate Hitler. The two generals arrived at Rommel's front door promptly at noon on October 14. They bore a message from the Führer.

Rommel had been implicated in the July 20 plot by

several known conspirators. Accordingly, Hitler was offering him the choice of standing trial for treason or of taking his own life by ingesting a poison caplet. If he opted to commit suicide, his family would be spared, and he would be given a hero's funeral. Rommel chose death by poison—"the officer's way."

■   ■   ■

After rounding the corner above Rommel's residence, the green Opel continued down the road toward the next village for about 200 yards. Burgdorf then ordered Heinrich Doose, the driver, to pull over. Doose later described what happened next:

> I had to get out, and General Maisel walked on up the road with me for some distance. After a while, about five or ten minutes, Burgdorf called us back to the car. I saw Rommel sitting in the back, obviously dying. He was unconscious, slumped down and sobbing—not a death rattle or groaning, but *sobbing*. His cap had fallen off. I sat him upright and put his cap back on.[128]

At 1:25 P.M. on October 14, 1944, Field Marshal Erwin Johannes Eugen Rommel was pronounced dead on arrival at Wagnerschule Reserve Hospital in Ulm. Onlookers who viewed his body observed a look of contempt on his face.

ENVOI

Hitler, from the heights of hypocrisy, ordered a state funeral for Rommel. It took place in Ulm on October 18. His remains were incinerated the next day and brought home for burial. There was no autopsy that might have revealed traces of poison—and of the sham perpetrated

Although Rommel was forced to take his own life in October 1944, Hitler agreed to spare his son and wife. Here, years later, Frau Rommel meets with surviving members of the Africa Corps.

by the Führer and his toadies. Rather than risk a public outcry, Hitler kept his promise and spared Lucie and Manfred Rommel.

Death came not proud to Rommel, whom many consider to have been one of the ten greatest generals of all time. He deserved far better than the humiliating end that fate decreed for him. In war, he fought fiercely but fairly; he was always a gentleman. In North Africa, he held back almost the entire weight of the British Empire for two years, while scribing an indelible place in the annals of history as the "Desert Fox." In peace, he was a devoted husband and a loving father. At all times, he was a patriot.

While the desert battles raged in Egypt, Libya, and Tunisia long ago, Rommel earned both the ire and admiration of Britain's prime minister. "We have a very skillful opponent against us," Winston Churchill declared, "and, may I say across the havoc of war, a great general."[129] Beyond victory, no soldier can ask for more than the respect of his enemy.

1891

November 15   Erwin Johannes Eugen Rommel is born in Heidenheim an der Brentz, Württemberg, Germany.

1910

July 19   Joins Imperial German Army's 124th Württemberg Infantry Regiment as officer cadet.

1912

January   Commisioned second lieutenant at *Kriegschule* (War Academy) in Danzig (now Gdansk, Poland).

1914

September 24   Awarded Iron Cross, Second Class.

1915

January 29   Awarded Iron Cross, First Class.

September   Promoted to first lieutenant.

1916

November 27   Marries Lucie Maria Mollin in Danzig.

1917

December 18   Awarded *Pour le Mérite*.

1918

January   Promoted to captain.

1929–1933   Posted as instructor at Infantry School, Dresden; writes *Infantry Attacks*.

1935–1937   Promoted to lieutenant colonel and assigned as instructor at War College, Potsdam; elevated to colonel.

1939

August–September Promoted to major general; serves as commander of Hitler's bodyguard during Polish campaign.

1940

February 15   Assumes command of Seventh Panzer Division.

May 26   Awarded Knight's Cross.

1941

January   Promoted to lieutenant general.

February 12   Arrives in Tripoli to command *Deutsches Afrika Korps*.

March 19   Awarded Oak Leaves to Knight's Cross.

July   Takes command of *Panzergruppe Afrika*.

1942

January 21 Elevated to colonel general in command of *Panzerarmee Afrika* and awarded Swords to Oak Leaves of Knight's Cross.

June 22 Promoted to field marshal.

1943

February 23 Assumes command of *Armeegruppe Afrika*.

March Receives Oak Leaves with Swords and Diamonds to Knight's Cross.

July 15 Appointed commander of Army Group B.

August 15 Establishes Army Group B headquarters in north Italy.

November 21 Army Group B headquarters moves to France.

1944

June–May Strengthens German defenses along Atlantic Wall.

June 6 D day in Normandy.

July 17 Critically injured in head when strafed by Allied fighter-bombers.

October 14 Ends own life by swallowing poison.

CHAPTER 1

1. Quoted in Erwin Rommel, *The Rommel Papers*. Edited by B. H. Liddell Hart, with Lucie-Maria Rommel, Manfred Rommel, and Fritz Bayerlein. Translated by Paul Findlay. New York: Da Capo Press, 1953, p. 502.
2. Ibid.
3. Ibid.
4. Ibid.
5. Quoted in David Irving, *Rommel: The Trail of the Fox*. Ware, Hertfordshire, UK: Wordsworth Editions, 1999, p. 403.
6. Ibid.
7. Ibid.
8. Ibid.
9. Ibid., p. 404.
10. Quoted in David Fraser, *Knight's Cross: A Life of Field Marshal Erwin Rommel*. New York: HarperCollins Publishers, 1994, p. 552.
11. Ibid., p. 550.

CHAPTER 2

12. Quoted in Irving, *Rommel*, p. 9.
13. Ibid., p. 10.
14. Ibid.
15. Quoted in Desmond Young, *Rommel: The Desert Fox*. New York: William Morrow, 1950, p. 15.
16. Young, *Rommel*, p. 15.
17. Quoted in Fraser, *Knight's Cross*, p. 28.
18. Ibid., p. 43.
19. Quoted in Irving, *Rommel*, p. 14.
20. Ibid., p. 15.
21. Ibid., p. 17.

CHAPTER 3

22. Quoted in Young, *Rommel*, pp. 29–30.
23. Quoted in Irving, *Rommel*, p. 21.
24. Quoted in Ian Kershaw, *Hitler, 1889–1936: Hubris*. New York: W. W. Norton, 1998, p. 424.
25. Quoted in Irving, *Rommel*, p. 35.
26. Quoted in Young, *Rommel*, p. 48.
27. Ibid.
28. Spencer C. Tucker, *Who's Who in Twentieth-Century Warfare*. New York: Routledge, 2001, p. 123.
29. Rommel, *The Rommel Papers*, p. 7.
30. Quoted in Young, *Rommel*, p. 49.
31. Quoted in Fraser, *Knight's Cross*, p. 170.
32. Quoted in Irving, *Rommel*, p. 42.
33. Ibid., p. 47.
34. Quoted in Martin Blumenson, "Rommel," in *Hitler's Generals*. Correlli Barnett, ed. New York: Quill/William Morrow, 1989, p. 299.
35. Quoted in Irving, *Rommel*, p. 48.
36. Quoted in Blumenson, "Rommel," p. 299.
37. Ibid., p. 298.
38. Quoted in Fraser, *Knight's Cross*, p. 191.
39. Ibid., p. 180.

CHAPTER 4

40. Rommel, *The Rommel Papers*, p. 98.
41. Quoted in Irving, *Rommel*, p. 59.
42. Quoted in Michael Veranov, ed., *The Mammoth Book of the Third Reich at War*. New York: Carroll & Graf, 1997, p. 252.
43. Ibid.
44. Ibid., p. 255.
45. Quoted in Blumenson, "Rommel," p. 301.
46. Quoted in Veranov, *The Mammoth Book of the Third Reich at War*, p. 262.
47. Ibid., p. 265.
48. Quoted in Blumenson, "Rommel," p. 301.
49. Quoted in Veranov, *The Mammoth Book of the Third Reich at War*, p. 269.
50. Ibid.
51. Quoted in Marcel Baudot, Henri Bernard, Hendrik Brugmans, Michael R. D. Foot, and Hans-Adolf Jacobsen, eds., *The Historical Encyclopedia of World War II*. Translated by Jesse Dilson. New York: Facts on File, 1980, p. 317.
52. Quoted in Veranov, *The Mammoth Book of the Third Reich at War*, p. 278.
53. Quoted in the Editors of Time-Life Books, *WWII: The Time-Life History of World War II*. New York: Barnes & Noble, 1995, p. 221.
54. Ibid.
55. Ibid.
56. Quoted in John Pimlott, ed., *The Hutchinson Atlas of Battle Plans: Before and After*. Oxford, UK: Helicon Publishing, 1998, p. 27.

CHAPTER 5

57. Rommel, *The Rommel Papers*, p. 293.
58. Ibid., p. 294.
59. Ibid., p. 295.
60. Ibid., p. 296.
61. Ibid., pp. 296–97.
62. Quoted in Irving, *Rommel*, p. 199.
63. Quoted in Blumenson, "Rommel," p. 305.
64. Quoted in Young, *Rommel*, p. 149.
65. Quoted in Irving, *Rommel*, p. 201.
66. Rommel, *The Rommel Papers*, p. 312.
67. Ibid., p. 315.
68. Ibid., p. 319.
69. Quoted in Irving, *Rommel*, p. 211.
70. Quoted in Veranov, *The Mammoth Book of the Third Reich at War*, p. 287.
71. Ibid.
72. Quoted in Pimlott, *The Hutchinson Atlas of Battle Plans*, p. 37.
73. Rommel, *The Rommel Papers*, p. 327.

CHAPTER 6

74. Quoted in the Editors of Time-Life Books, *WWII*, p. 223.
75. Quoted in Rommel, *The Rommel Papers*, p. 337.
76. Rommel, *The Rommel Papers*, p. 358.
77. Quoted in Irving, *Rommel*, p. 225.
78. Ibid.
79. Quoted in Young, *Rommel*, p. 155.
80. Ibid.
81. Ibid.
82. Ibid.
83. Ibid., p. 156.
84. Quoted in Omar N. Bradley and Clay Blair, *A General's Life: An Autobiography by General of the Army Omar N. Bradley and Clay Blair.* New York: Simon & Schuster, 1983, p. 123.
85. Quoted in Irving, *Rommel*, p. 236.
86. Rommel, *The Rommel Papers*, p. 394.
87. Ibid., p. 398.
88. Ibid.
89. Ibid., p. 402.
90. Quoted in the Editors of Time-Life Books, *WWII*, p. 224.
91. Rommel, *The Rommel Papers*, p. 407.
92. Quoted in Blumenson, "Rommel," p. 308.

CHAPTER 7

93. Rommel, *The Rommel Papers*, p. 422.
94. Quoted in Blumenson, "Rommel," p. 308.
95. Rommel, *The Rommel Papers*, p. 422.
96. Ibid.
97. Quoted in Irving, *Rommel*, p. 279.
98. Ibid., p. 284.
99. Quoted in Norman Polmar and Thomas B. Allen, eds., *World War II: The Encyclopedia of the War Years 1941–1945.* New York: Random House, 1996, p. 111.
100. Quoted in Irving, *Rommel*, p. 287.
101. Quoted in Samuel W. Mitcham, Jr., *The Desert Fox in Normandy: Rommel's Defense of Fortress Europe.* Westport, CT: Praeger, 1997, p. 11.
102. Quoted in Irving, *Rommel*, pp. 285–86.
103. Quoted in Mitcham, *The Desert Fox in Normandy*, p. 5.
104. Max Pemsel, "Seventh Army, June 1942–6 June 1944: Report of the Chief of Staff," in Günther Blumentritt, Wilhelm Keitel, Alfred Jodl, et al., *Fighting the Invasion: The German Army at D-Day.* Edited by David C. Isby. Mechanicsburg, PA: Stackpole Books, 2000, pp. 62–63.
105. Quoted in Irving, *Rommel*, p. 336.
106. Quoted in Sidney C. Moody, Jr., and the Associated Press, *War in Europe.* Novato, CA: Presidio Press, 1993, p. 133.
107. Ibid.

108. Quoted in the Editors of Time-Life Books, *WWII*, p. 301.
109. Ibid.
110. Quoted in Blumenson, "Rommel," p. 312.
111. Quoted in the Editors of Time-Life Books, *WWII*, p. 301.
112. Quoted in Fraser, *Knight's Cross*, p. 507.
113. Ibid.
114. Ibid.
115. Ibid.

CHAPTER 8

116. Quoted in Young, *Rommel*, p. 187.
117. Quoted in Fraser, *Knight's Cross*, p. 515.
118. Quoted in Mitcham, *The Desert Fox in Normandy*, p. 186.
119. Ibid., pp. 189–90.
120. Quoted in Georges Blond, "The Plot to Kill Hitler," in Reader's Digest Association, *Reader's Digest Illustrated Story of World War II.* Pleasantville, NY: Reader's Digest Association, 1978, p. 385.
121. Quoted in Mitcham, *The Desert Fox in Normandy*, p. 191.
122. Ibid., p. 190.
123. Ibid., p. 192.
124. Quoted in Irving, *Rommel*, p. 397.
125. Ibid.
126. Quoted in Mitcham, *The Desert Fox in Normandy*, p. 192.
127. Ibid., p. 196.
128. Quoted in Irving, *Rommel*, p. 405.
129. Quoted in Vincent B. Hawkins, "Erwin Rommel [1891–1944]," in *Brassey's Encyclopedia of Land Forces and Warfare.* Edited by Franklin D. Margiotta. Washington, DC: Brassey's, 1996, p. 812.

Alexander, Bevin. *How Great Generals Win*. New York: W. W. Norton, 2002.

Barnett, Correlli, ed. *Hitler's Generals*. New York: Quill/William Morrow, 1989.

Baudot, Marcel, Henri Bernard, Hendrik Brugmans, Michael R. D. Foot, and Hans-Adolf Jacobsen, eds. *The Historical Encyclopedia of World War II*. Translated by Jesse Dilson. New York: Facts on File, 1980.

Blumentritt, Günther, Wilhelm Keitel, Alfred Jodl, et al. *Fighting the Invasion: The German Army at D-Day*. Edited by David C. Isby. Mechanicsville, PA: Stackpole Books, 2000.

Bradley, Omar N., and Clay Blair. *A General's Life: An Autobiography by General of the Army Omar N. Bradley and Clay Blair*. New York: Simon & Schuster, 1983.

Chant, Christopher, ed. *Warfare and the Third Reich: The Rise and Fall of Hitler's Armed Forces*. New York: Smithmark Publishers, 1996.

Cooper, Matthew. *The German Army, 1939–1945: Its Political and Military Failure*. Military Book Club edition. USA: Scarborough House, (undated).

Davis, Paul K. *100 Decisive Battles: From Ancient Times to the Present*. New York: Oxford University Press, 1999.

Dear, C. B., and M. R. D. Foot, eds. *The Oxford Companion to World War II*. New York: Oxford University Press, 1995.

Dupuy, Ernest, and Trevor Dupuy. *The Encyclopedia of Military History: From 3500 B.C. to the Present*. Rev. ed. New York: Harper & Row, 1986.

Dupuy, Trevor N., Curt Johnson, and David L. Bongard. *The Harper Encyclopedia of Military Biography*. New York: HarperCollins, 1992.

Editors of Time-Life Books. *WW II: The Time-Life History of World War II*. New York: Barnes & Noble, 1995.

Eggenberger, David. *An Encyclopedia of Battles: Accounts of over 1,560 Battles from 1479 B.C. to the Present*. New York: Dover Publications, 1985.

Ellis, John. *The Military Book Club's World War II: The Encyclopedia of Facts and Figures*. N.p., 1995.

Fest, Joachim. *Plotting Hitler's Death: The Story of the German Resistance*. Translated by Bruce Little. New York: Henry Holt, 1996.

Fraser, David. *Knight's Cross: A Life of Field Marshal Erwin Rommel*. New York: HarperCollins Publishers, 1994.

Gardiner, Juliet. *D-Day: Those Who Were There*. London: Collins & Brown, 1994.

Irving, David. *Rommel: The Trail of the Fox*. Ware, Hertfordshire, UK: Wordsworth Editions, 1999.

Kershaw, Ian. *Hitler, 1936–1945: Nemesis*. New York: W. W. Norton, 2000.

Lucas, James. *Hitler's Enforcers: Leaders of the German War Machine 1939–1945*. London: Arms and Armour Press, 1996.

————. *Battle Group! German Kampfgruppen Action of World War Two*. London: Arms and Armour Press, 1993.

Margiotta, Franklin D., ed. *Brassey's Encyclopedia of Military History and Biography*. Washington, DC: Brassey's, 1994.

Mitcham, Samuel W. Jr. *Triumphant Fox: Erwin Rommel and the Rise of the* Afrika Korps. New York: Cooper Square Press, 2000.

————. *The Desert Fox in Normandy: Rommel's Defense of Fortress Europe*. Westport, CT: Praeger, 1997.

Moody, Sidney C. Jr., and the Associated Press. *War in Europe*. Novato, CA: Presidio Press, 1993.

Perrett, Bryan. *The Battle Book: Crucial Conflicts in History from 1469 B.C. to the Present*. London: Arms and Armour Press, 1992.

Pimlott, John, ed. *The Hutchinson Atlas of Battle Plans: Before and After*. Oxford, UK: Helicon Publishing, 1998.

Polmar, Norman, and Thomas B. Allen, eds. *World War II: The Encyclopedia of the War Years 1941–1945*. New York: Random House, 1996.

Reader's Digest Association. *Reader's Digest Illustrated Story of World War II*. Pleasantville, NY: Reader's Digest Association, 1978.

Rolf, David. *The Bloody Road to Tunis: Destruction of the Axis Forces in North Africa, November 1942–May 1943*. Mechanicsburg, PA: Stackpole Books, 2001.

Rommel, Erwin. *The Rommel Papers*. Edited by B. H. Liddell Hart with Lucie-Maria Rommel, Manfred Rommel, and Fritz Bayerlein. Translated by Paul Findlay. New York: Da Capo Press, 1953.

Tucker, Spencer C. *Who's Who in Twentieth-Century Warfare*. New York: Routledge, 2001.

Veranov, Michael, ed. *The Mammoth Book of the Third Reich at War*. New York: Carroll & Graf, 1997.

Wheal, Elizabeth-Anne, Stephen Pope, and James Taylor. *Encyclopedia of the Second World War*. Edison, NJ: Castle Books, 1989.

Young, Desmond. *Rommel: The Desert Fox*. New York: William Morrow, 1950.

Young, Peter. *A Dictionary of Battles (1816–1976)*. New York: Mayflower Books, 1978.

Ambrose, Stephen E. *The Victors, Eisenhower and His Boys: The Men of World War II*. New York: Simon & Schuster, 1998.

———. *Citizen Soldiers: The U.S. Army from the Normandy Beaches to the Bulge to the Surrender of Germany: June 7, 1944–May 7, 1945*. New York: Simon & Schuster, 1997.

———. *D-Day, June 6, 1944: The Climactic Battle of World War II*. New York: Simon & Schuster, 1994.

———. *Band of Brothers: E Company, 506th Regiment, 101st Airborne: From Normandy to Hitler's Eagle's Nest*. New York: Simon & Schuster, 1992.

Ambrose, Stephen E., and C. L. Sulzberger. *American Heritage New History of World War II*. New York: Viking, 1997.

Badsey, Stephen. *Normandy 1944: Allied Landings and Breakout*. Campaign Series, edited by David G. Chandler. Botley, Oxford, UK: Osprey, 1999.

Carell, Paul. *Invasion—They're Coming! The German Account of the Allied Landings and the 80 Days' Battle for France*. New York: E. P. Dutton, 1963.

Chandler, David G. *Battles and Battlescenes of World War Two*. New York: Macmillan, 1989.

Chandler, David G., Colin McIntyre, and Michael C. Tagg. *Chronicles of World War II*. Godalming, Surrey, UK: 1997.

Churchill, Winston. *Closing the Ring*. Vol. 5 of *The Second World War*. Boston: Houghton Mifflin, 1951.

———. *The Grand Alliance*. Vol. 4 of *The Second World War*. Boston: Houghton Mifflin, 1950.

Congdon, Don, ed. *Combat World War II: Europe*. New York: Galahad Books, 1996.

Cowley, Robert, ed. *No End Save Victory: Perspectives on World War II*. New York: G. P. Putnam's Sons, 2001.

D'Este, Carlo. *Eisenhower: A Soldier's Life*. New York: Henry Holt, 2002.

———. *Decision at Normandy*. New York: HarperCollins, 1994.

Dunnigan, James F., and Albert A. Nofi. *Dirty Little Secrets of World War II: Military Information No One Told You about the Greatest, Most Terrible War in History*. New York: William Morrow, 1994.

Eisenhower, Dwight D. *Crusade in Europe*. Baltimore, MD: Johns Hopkins University Press, 1997.

Flower, Desmond, and James Reeves, eds. *The War, 1939–1945: A Documentary History*. New York: Da Capo Press, 1997.

Gilbert, Martin. *The Second World War: A Complete History*. New York: Henry Holt, 1989.

Gill, Anton. *An Honourable Defeat: A History of the German Resistance to Hitler, 1933–1945*. New York: Henry Holt, 1994.

Goldstein, Richard. *America at D-Day: A Book of Remembrance*. New York: Delta/Bantam Doubleday Dell, 1994.

Hanson, Victor Davis. *The Soul of Battle: From Ancient Times to the Present Day, How Three Great Liberators Vanquished Tyranny*. New York: Free Press, 1999.

Hogg, Ian V. *The Hutchinson Dictionary of Battles*. Oxford, UK: Helicon Publishing, 1998.

Keegan, John, ed. *The Book of War*. New York: Viking, 1999.

Kershaw, Ian. *Hitler, 1889–1936: Hubris*. New York: W. W. Norton, 1998.

Kilvert-Jones, Tim. *Omaha Beach: V Corps' Battle for the Normandy Beachhead*. Battleground Europe Series. Barnsley, UK: Leo Cooper/Pen & Sword Books, 1999.

Leckie, Robert. *The Wars of America*. Vol. 2: *From 1900 to 1992*. New York: HarperCollins, 1992.

Lewis, Jon E., ed. *The Mammoth Book of Battles*. New York: Carroll & Graf, 1995.

———. *Eye-Witness D-Day: The Story of the Battle by Those Who Were There*. New York: Carroll & Graf, 1994.

MacDonald, Charles B. *The Mighty Endeavor: The American War in Europe*. New York: Da Capo Press, 1992.

Mansoor, Peter R. *The GI Offensive in Europe: The Triumph of American Infantry Divisions, 1941–1945*. Lawrence, KS: University Press of Kansas, 1999.

Margiotta, Franklin D., ed. *Brassey's Encyclopedia of Land Forces and Warfare*. Washington, DC: Brassey's, 1996.

Messenger, Charles. *Sepp Dietrich: Hitler's Gladiator: The Life and Times of Oberstgruppenführer and Panzergeneral-Oberst der Waffen SS Sepp Dietrich*. London: Brassey's Defence Publishers, 1988.

Morison, Samuel Eliot. *The Invasion of France and Germany, 1944–1945*. Vol. 11 of *History of United States Naval Operations in World War II*. Edison, NJ: Castle Books, 2001.

Murray, Williamson, and Allan R. Millett. *A War to Be Won: Fighting the Second World War*. Cambridge, MA: Belknap Press of Harvard University Press, 2000.

Overy, Richard. *Why the Allies Won*. New York: W.W. Norton, 1996.

Ryan, Cornelius. *The Longest Day: June 6, 1944*. New York: Simon & Schuster, 1959.

Shilleto, Carl. *Utah Beach, St Mère Église*. Battleground Europe Series. Barnsley, UK: Leo Cooper/Pen & Sword Books, 2001.

Weinberg, Gerhard L. *A World at Arms: A Global History of World War II*. New York: Cambridge University Press, 1994.

Wilson, Theodore A., ed. *D-Day 1944*. Lawrence, KS: University Press of Kansas, 1994.

page:

11: © Bettmann/CORBIS
14: © CORBIS
17: Library of Congress/
   lc-dig-ppmsca-00753
20: © Bettmann/CORBIS
23: © Hulton-Deutsch Collection/
   CORBIS
29: ©Bettmann/CORBIS
33: Associated Press, AP
37: Associated Press, AP
40: © CORBIS
43: Associated Press, AP
47: Associated Press, AP
50: Associated Press, AP
54: Associated Press, AP
57: © Bettmann/CORBIS

62: © CORBIS
64: Associated Press, AP
67: Associated Press, AP
72: Associated Press, AP
75: © CORBIS
78: © CORBIS
82: © Bettmann/CORBIS
85: Associated Press, AP
88: Associated Press, AP
93: Associated Press, AP
97: ©Hulton-Deutsch Collection/
   CORBIS
101: © CORBIS
104: ©Hulton-Deutsch Collection/
   CORBIS

Cover: © CORBIS
Frontis: Associated Press, AP

EARLE RICE JR. is a former senior design engineer and technical writer in the aerospace industry. After serving nine years with the U.S. Marine Corps, he attended San Jose City College and Foothill College on the San Francisco Peninsula. He has devoted full time to his writing since 1993 and has written more than forty books for young adults. Earle is a member of the Society of Children's Book Writers and Illustrators; the League of World War I Aviation Historians and its UK-based sister organization, Cross & Cockade International, the United States Naval Institute, and the Air Force Association.

CASPAR W. WEINBERGER was the fifteenth secretary of defense, serving under President Ronald Reagan from 1981 to 1987. Born in California in 1917, he fought in the Pacific during World War II then went on to pursue a law career. He became an active member of the California Republican Party and was named the party's chairman in 1962. Over the next decade, Weinberger held several federal government offices, including chairman of the Federal Trade Commission and secretary of health, education, and welfare. Ronald Reagan appointed him to be secretary of defense in 1981.

During his years at the Pentagon, Weinberger worked to protect the United States against the Soviet Union, which many people at the time perceived as the greatest threat to America. He became one of the most respected secretaries of defense in history and served longer than any previous secretary except for Robert McNamara (who served 1961–1968). Today, Weinberger is chairman of the influential *Forbes* magazine.